A ROYAL
LOVE
Revealed

....

MY JOURNEY FROM
SORROW TO GOD'S HEART

♥

Published by Sharpehouse
csharpehouse@gmail.com

Library of Congress Control Number: 2016920435
ISBN: 978-0-692-78672-7

Heart Photography by Corrine Sharpe
Editorial by Kimberly Smith Ashley kmsmithwrites.com
Cover photo by istock.com
Scripture taken from the King James Version, which is in the public domain.

Printed in the United States of America

DEDICATION

♥

Dedicated to my loving, beautiful mother.
Your love and God's love live on in the next generations of our family
because of your faithfulness in sharing our value in Jesus.

For my best friend and husband, Erik.
I'm forever grateful for your devotion and love to me and our children.
You are the love of my youth and forever more.

To our two children, Hayden and Loren.
You bring such joy and love to our family, for you are our reward.

And I will give them a heart to know me, that I am the Lord;
and they shall be my people, and I will be their God: for they shall
return unto me with their whole heart.

- Jeremiah 24:7 KJV

♥

TABLE OF CONTENTS

PREFACE

I began the journey of writing a book not because I am a writer, but because I experienced hope, beauty, and joy out of excruciating pain. I do not feel equipped to tell a story of any kind. I have written A Royal Love Revealed out of obedience to a God who called me out to do it and gave me everything I needed to complete the task he asked of me. It was through baby steps, plenty of patience, and total reliance upon God. I haven't always been very good at patience, but I am learning that in the waiting is where the goodness of God happens. It is also where we have this exchange with the Father and learn how to communicate and have a dialogue with him, have moments with him, and finally, how to trust him with everything we have.

I lost one of the closest people to my heart, my mom. She was everything to me. She was the picture of love and grace. If we weren't together, she was just a phone call away. My mother knew me the most, and she told me the truth no matter what. Most important, she taught me the value of self-worth and the value of a life lived with Jesus at its center. Cancer ended her earthly life at an early age. Mom gained eternity in February 2011. In my pain and sorrow, I cried out to the God I had known since I was eleven years old. I had dropped off my two young children at school and was driving down the interstate. In my moment of surrender, I cried and asked God to come so close to me that I could feel him ever so strongly in my grieving. I told him that I needed him here with me!

In a still, small voice, God spoke to me. "Look for the hearts," he said. What? I asked myself, Good hearts of other people? Your love around me? Actual hearts? As I continued down the interstate, still puzzled, I glanced up at the sky, and there was a perfect heart shape in the clouds. I rubbed my eyes and said to myself, There is no way! I looked repeatedly. Yes, it was a heart. In my amazement, I shared

this with the people closest to me, my husband, children, frie[...] and family. Since this day, we have all been overcome with the [...] pernatural, eternal love of a good Heavenly Father through see[...] hearts when and where you would never dream of seeing th[...]

A Royal Love Revealed is a collection of hearts that tells a story, a st[...] of real love that never leaves you the same. Am I loved? Am I valua[...] The world we live in has its ideas and opinions of what love is [...] who or what is valuable. I present to you that your value comes f[...] within. It is inherent, from being made in the image of Love. Thro[...] moments and powerful imagery, you will see for yourself that coi[...] dence has nothing to do with it. It is the unexplainable at work. C[...] desires to walk with us in relationship and show us his unwavering l[...]

These stunning photos tell my story and the story of my belo[...] friends and family that God is with us and for us. This message is a p[...] of a greater story for all of humanity—that Jesus gave his life to g[...] you life here and now and for eternity. His love is unshakable, w[...] and all consuming. There is no greater love than the love of the Fat[...]

My prayer is that this book will show you that God confirms you[...] all that he calls you to do, and that through life's most painful tim[...] he does bring good out of it, if we will seek him and trust him[...] you will turn your heart to his heart, you will beat as one, in rhyt[...] together.

His love covers everything with beauty. It lets us breathe again a[...] gives wings to our hearts after we have experienced the pains and l[...] of this fallen world. If we have eyes to see his beauty right before u[...] is life changing. He is a living God, and his word is active and alive a[...] breathes life to all things in our world when we believe it and speak[...]

WHAT THE ENEMY BRINGS FOR DESTRUCTION, GOD TURNS FOR GOOD. HIS GRACE GIVES US THE STRENGTH TO RECEIVE THIS FIERCE, CONSUMING, RELENTLESS LOVE THAT WE DID NOT EARN.

♥

This scripture explains so well the exchange with our Father in heaven. Jeremiah 24:7 says, "And I will give them a heart to know me, that I am the Lord; and they shall be my people, and I will be their God: for they shall return unto me with their whole heart." He has the power to give us a heart to receive him, make our heart whole, and show others his love. We are but mere man: however, through the power of Christ, we are royal and able to extend a love that lasts for eternity. We are able to experience the one true living God in a relationship.

What the enemy brings for destruction, God turns for good. His grace gives us the strength to receive this fierce, consuming, relentless love that we did not earn. Moreover, his grace supplies us with the ability to overcome this life's challenges. It is the kind of love that leaves you breathless and forever changed. From the pit of your stomach, you know who you belong to when you experience Christ. You also realize that there is a bigger plan at work than simply attaining earthly possessions or status. It is counterculture, but it is the freedom trail to a vastness we can't contain in our human minds.

SPECIAL THANKS

I would like to give special thanks to my friends and family
who encouraged me through these uncharted waters.
Your hearts are such a beautiful representation of our Father in heaven.
You make the journey of this life sweeter and richer because of your love and friendship.
Also, I wish to thank a dear friend who exemplifies that
when you lay down your life for a brother, you truly find your life.

INTRODUCTION

The story begins with a little girl who grew up with an emotionally unavailable mother and father in a family riddled with physical, emotional, and alcohol abuse. That girl was my mom. She would be gripped with fear when her father would come home in a drunken state. He was physically abusive to her mother. Fear grew in their household as the cycle of poverty and abuse continued. Growing up, my mom was never encouraged to discover who she was in Christ, and she felt a great deal of oppression and control from her mother most of her life. She knew it was only her mother repeating the patterns of behaviors she'd experienced as a child, but those patterns do their damage to a person's soul and spirit. It affected my mom until her last days. When we are not willing to lay down our pride and fear, we ignore God calling us to his best for us. God's best for us is the way of peace and healing. The truth is sometimes painful, yes, but it always brings healing afterward.

As my mom grew up, she wrestled with regret and felt she missed out on relationships and opportunities because her mom, acting out of fear, would refuse to let her do or participate in much of anything. There was no discussion. This continued even as my mom became a young adult and was still living with her mom. Fortunately, there was someone my mom could talk to and from whom she could feel unconditional love. God always makes the way of escape for those who seek him and have pure hearts before him. God gave that little girl, my mom, an example of love through an aunt. When my mom felt depleted by her circumstances, her aunt filled her up again. She taught her about the Lord and showed her unconditional love. It would help my mom become such a loving parent by showing unconditional love and teaching her children about God's love for them, and it showed wisdom when she broke the negative family cycles.

Later in life, choosing a partner that was equally yoked or like minded was difficult for my mom. She still had not healed from the emotional wounds of her childhood. Despite her marrying husband similar to her father, she still managed to impart God's love and knowledge to her three children and to many others as well. Faithfully, she clung to God's word and continued to seek his wisdom in all things. She filled the roles of both mother and father to her children.

Through obedience and relationship, God shatters statistics and worldly dictates about a person's circumstances. Breaking free from the world's expectations and entering the adventurous realm without boundaries brings us back to our first love in complete wholeness. As with anything worthwhile, it requires effort, dedication, and turning away from toxic thoughts and situations. God is a God of order. Without it, we would have chaos.

God's word is truth. We need that truth so that we can determine when we are faced with a lie. God has plans for his children. He does not want to harm us but enable us to prosper.

Inevitably, people will let us down. Many times, it is beyond our control, especially when we are children. Whereas, if you are fixed on Christ, he can break every statistic and stereotype that the world attempts to place on you as you follow him. From a statistics standpoint, every one of them was broken for me and my siblings. We would not grow up to be alcoholics, drug addicts, abusers, depressed, or adulterers. When you belong to him, you are royal and set apart for his works. It has everything to do with trust and sacrifice and not being elevated above others or given special treatment. My mom was a beautiful example of serving others and pouring into others while

GOD'S WORD IS TRUTH. WE NEED THAT TRUTH SO THAT WE CAN DETERMINE WHEN WE ARE FACED WITH A LIE.

♥

she had learned about this over-the-top, loving God, this God that has no limits.

Every year at Christmas time, my mom would decorate our Christmas tree with heart-themed lights and ornaments. She would explain to us that this is what Christmas is all about, the love of Christ! Every greeting card she gave for any occasion would always include a heart, either on the card itself or drawn by her hand. She even wore heart jewelry. She was passionate about this message.

My mom was a forgiving and long-suffering woman in many ways. She was not perfect but her heart was always open to God. My mom was my best friend. We did everything together. I knew that if I ever wanted an honest opinion from her that is what I would get. Her strength shined through my entire life, even in the hardest of times. She still had her own personal struggles, as do we all, but that is what is beautiful about our relationship with God: We don't have to be perfect. We only have to seek to know him and to realize that he is our loving Father who gives us hope and moves all things for our good. We are to encourage each other and let each other know that we are not alone.

My mom is the most generous person I know. She gave me a profound sense of self-worth and rich understanding of God's truths. Continually, she helped and served others, giving her time, talent, money, and encouragement to anyone who needed it, no matter who they were. She brought some of her children's friends to the Lord, among other people, including all three of her children's spouses. Hearts have been symbolic since my birth. I didn't make the connection until I was writing this book, but my mother's father gave me a gold heart locket when I was born. He had been divorced from my

grandmother for a very long time and did not come around often. He was also an alcoholic and not really a part of my mother's life, so this gift took her by surprise. She also always wore a heart locket. It was the last piece of jewelry she would wear. Mom gave it to me when she went into the hospital for the last time before she passed into eternity. In the summer of 2010, my mom was diagnosed with breast cancer that had spread to her bone. When my mom could no longer care for herself, we opened our home to care for her. My husband and I didn't think twice about it. After all, this was the woman who not only raised me, but also taught both of us so much about a relationship with Jesus and our value in his eyes. This was my sweet mother, who gave her very best to me, my brothers, and our families.

My husband had a wonderful relationship with my mom and was always supportive of my family. He had known my mom since he was eighteen years old. She had been a person of strength for him in his walk with the Lord. I am very grateful for my husband's love, support, and generous spirit. He had to share his time with me as I cared for my mom, and he never complained, not one time. He saw the bigger picture and knew that love sometimes means sacrifice. My husband also knew that when it is God's will that God will ultimately give back to us more than we can imagine because of our trust and faithfulness to his works. My mom moved into our home that summer, and I took care of her while she fought her second bout of cancer. She had beaten colon cancer three years prior.

I was a stay-at-home mom with one child in preschool three days a week and another in elementary school. My oldest was playing flag football and basketball throughout the year. We lived a normal, middle-class American lifestyle. I continued to volunteer in multiple

HIS MESSAGE WAS THAT OF HIS LOVE FOR HIS PEOPLE AND THAT HIS HEART FIRST LOVED US BEFORE WE EVER HAD THE ABILITY TO LOVE.

♥

outreaches at our church and lead small groups for teen girls in foster care, but as my mom grew weaker and needed more care, some of those things had to be put on the back burner temporarily. I still continued with the girls' outreach because it was something that invigorated me and gave me encouragement. I was given a special assignment to love the one who gave me life. It was a sacred time and a time for myself and my husband and two small children to love her unconditionally.

My heart was broken that her husband did not make the choice to care for her the way she needed and deserved to be cared for. Before she came to us, she would be left alone while getting sick from cancer treatments, feeling very lonely and hurt. No one was there to help her clean up and get comfortable again after dealing with the side effects from medications. Her modality was compromised due to the cancer spreading to her hip, and she eventually could not eat due to the cancer also spreading to her intestines. As a result, she was placed on liquid nutrition through an IV. God spoke to my heart that this was my mission to care for my mom, which I felt that I was doing already, but now it would be in a deeper way, pushing everything else aside. This proved to be no easy task, having to provide for my two young children's daily needs while trying to maintain some sense of normalcy and continued joy and peace in our home.

My day would consist of waking up early to help Mom clean up and give her fluids. I was so scared that I would do something improperly, causing her more pain or discomfort. It was challenging, to say the least, to learn how to prepare, clean, and administer nutrition through

an IV. I felt ill equipped and in way over my head. I would pray every time before I would begin, calling out to the God I knew and loved, all the while knowing that I could not do anything without his help, that is greater than my capabilities. God gave me the knowledge and grace. I never felt that more than when I was helping Mom. As hard as it was some days, it was the most fulfilling thing I have ever done.

To be totally honest, there were some days I missed fun opportunities I would normally have experienced with my kids. Going to the beach, playing with friends, and enjoying day trips were all put on the back burner at this time, but God gives us the grace and ability to have joy and to stay in an attitude of gratitude in the moment. Jesus gave us this example when he walked the earth. No matter how hard some days would be just from the weight of responsibility, tasks, and physical exhaustion, he would revive me with his love and presence in my life as I continued to seek him. .

One of the special joys was when we would do story time before bed for the kids, all together in Mom's room. We would all pile in her room and talk or play board games. My littlest one would watch her favorite TV shows with Mom. One special night, the kids dressed up and put together a parade, marching through Mom's room singing and dancing.

Before Mom got really sick, we would sit outside and watch the kids play while we listened to music and enjoyed the simple pleasures of nature. We welcomed these carefree respites, as we were dealing with not only my mom's health, but also an enormous amount of added stress due to trying to navigate through Mom's finances

deal with the lack of support from her husband. Nothing is
se in this life than a lack of care from loved ones. It brings on
a dark hopelessness that leaves one feeling sick, forgotten,
mportant, and of little value. I found it very difficult to com-
hend this lack of care on her husband's part. Some days I felt
t in my stomach from the deception from my stepparent, the
d of deception that chokes out peace and takes your breath away.

children of God, we are not meant to be under these dark veils of
elessness and negativity. This clearly runs counter to the incred-
love of our Father expressed through his people. You see and
the vast difference of how God intended for life to be before
world became a sinful place. We identify with goodness and
, not the darkness and deception that steals our peace and joy.

had regular doctor appointments at multiple hospitals, and
would take my young children with us. The kids and I would
ke frequent visits to the doctor's office to pick up prescrip-
ns or anything else that was needed.

e day her primary doctor looked at me and said, "Look at you,
king up here with a smile on your face, kids in tow, going all about."

ld her that it was all thanks to God. I didn't have the strength
hout him. With God, however, the impossible becomes possible.
on't want to sound cliché but it's that simple. I can do nothing
ger than myself, nor can I have joy, love, peace, understanding,
ience, self-control, forgiveness, or kindness without God liv-
inside me and me relying on him to fill me up each day as I
k and honor him. He truly gives us the strength to move the
untains in our lives. Keeping everything positive in our home
m the music, movies, prayers, worshiping together as a fam-
and daily devotion and quiet time with Jesus, all helped me
y in his freedom and presence, ready to tackle the day's tasks.

e have so many material and earthly pleasures before us in our
rld, but choosing our Father's best, really is freeing, encourag-
g, and exciting! Moreover, when we read God's living word and
e the moments each day to be still and focus on him, it chang-
how we see and prioritize the things around us. God meets us
ere we are. Some days my mom and I just needed a good cry.
e were praying and believing and hoping for her to be healed of
s disease, but God had different plans. I knew in my heart that
gain heaven is everything, no matter if it is when we would
e it to happen or not. She was healed in heaven and in para-
e with her King. What a beautifully glorious place to be how
was before our world became fallen in the Garden of Eden.

y mom went into eternity in February 2011. That day, when I was
ving on the interstate, in my moment of surrender and crying out to
od, asking him to come closer because I was heartbroken and needed
n. He responded to me in a still, small voice, "Look for the hearts."
hat? I questioned what I'd heard. Was I to look for the good heart in
ers? Was I to look for God's love around me? Actual hearts? Then,

as I continued down the interstate, glancing up at the sky, I witnessed
a perfect heart shape in the clouds—that was my watershed moment.
In my amazement, I shared this story with my mom's dear friend
who'd helped me care for Mom during those eight months. A few
days later, we were driving through a neighborhood with a detour,
and she said, "Look, Corrine. You're missing it!" I looked up at the
detour sign as I was turning, and there was a pink heart spray-
painted on the detour sign. At that very moment, we had been talking about Mom, the past few weeks, and what God had spoken
to me about the hearts. She looked at me and said, "That is God!"

A week later, I was driving down the road not thinking about anything
in particular, and as I looked up, I again saw a heart in the clouds. I
was both shocked and comforted. The week after that, I was driving
home and, again a third time, I looked up to see a heart in the clouds.
Later that week, while I was taking my morning walk down my
favorite stretch of woods, I found myself missing Mom and thinking about her, so I began to pray to God for strength and understanding. Yet again, God showed me heart-shaped clouds. I thought
this was incredible. It was so intimate and loving of my Father in
heaven. I could not contain my tears. I could not deny what he was
doing. All I could think was that God is so present and so loving.

My mom possessed so much love and wisdom, even though she did
not have anyone to give it consistently to her. She was found and
given everything she needed in his presence by the Holy Spirit. She
was truly a student of God's word and a seeker of the Father's heartbeat. My mother continues to speak to my heart, the very truth of life.

The truth and God's grace, led by the Holy Spirit, is the only way to
help people find their true love, their heavenly Father.

God gently spoke to my heart and told me that I needed to start
taking pictures of all the hearts I was seeing so that I could share
them with others. Further along in this journey, the Lord told
me to include the pictures in a book with a message that he had
for his children. With God, it is always about everyone, not just
one. His message was that of his love for his people and that
his heart first loved us before we ever had the ability to love. I
think of 1 John 4:19: "We love him, because he first loved us."

This process drew me closer to him and his heart than anything ever has before in my life. My childhood was not an easy
one. However, I look back and see how faithful God is and how
he can make something out of very little. It is what he does. I am
the first born of three in my family. My father and mother grew
up in alcoholic families where there was abuse of every kind.

My dad grew up in a family where he was left to fend for himself. His
mother was focused on this world's pleasures and not his well-being.
His father left his family. These early traumas left my father with
emotionally unavailable parents. My dad's oldest sister shouldered
much of the responsibility in their family. She was there for him and
his other brother as much as she could be. She continues to be a

beautiful example of a loving, selfless, kind-hearted presence in both my life as well as my brother's life. She and my uncle were there for us when we were children and my dad passed away.

My father was unfaithful to my mother. He also abused alcohol and drugs. There were many emotional hurts and trespasses of trust in their marriage. When someone is not in their right mind, you experience emotional abuse due to their choices. It got to be too much for my mom, and my parents divorced after ten years of marriage.

I will never forget the day my father moved out and I learned they were getting a divorce. At age five, I was heartbroken and mad. My brother had just been born. I could not imagine what was wrong with my father. Why couldn't he be everything I needed him to be as a loving father who was there for me?

It saddens me to say that I only have a handful of memories of him: various fragments of different moments pieced together. Some of them I remember as good, but one of them was pretty terrifying. I remember fishing with my dad and going to the zoo. Those were the good memories. Pictures helped me piece together more about my childhood when my parents were married.

The terrifying memory was one in which my father came home drunk and began yelling at my mother over something trivial. I was sitting on the couch and he took off his belt. It had a large buckle on the end. He swung the belt and it hit me in the head. My mom panicked, of course, and immediately tried to calm him down. I ran to my room, crying, my world shattered. I couldn't believe the man I saw as my hero did such a terrible thing. He eventually came to my room and apologized, but it didn't make me feel any better. I never looked at him the same again. After that, trusting him was extremely difficult.

I was never fortunate enough to know the joy of having a loving father. Thankfully, though, my mother had a heart for the Lord and taught her children all she learned about this loving God. She was a woman of constant prayer. Those prayers and trust in God is what brought us through many hard times growing up and gave us a hope and a future.

My dad committed suicide when I was ten years old. I remember not knowing what to feel. I hadn't seen him in two years because of his life choices, and then I saw him just a week before he passed. My brother and I went fishing with him, and then the three of us went to lunch together.

My dad's death was one of the most difficult things I have ever had to comprehend in my life at such a young age, but God met me there. I am so grateful that no matter how broken our family life became that I had a mother that pointed me to Jesus. Adults can carry so much that it sometimes overwhelms them, but if we truly take time to know God, he will carry it all for us. He will make our burden light and heal our broken hearts. Matthew 11:30 says, "For my yoke is easy, and my burden is light." He gives rest for our weary souls.

I never knew a man that lived for Christ in my life, but I knew wh[at I] didn't want! And sometimes that's just as good of an example to [help] guide us. I would continue to learn more about Jesus and grow in [my] walk with him. Sometimes I would completely fail, but I would alw[ays] get back up and start again, allowing his light and truth to restore [me.]

I had many responsibilities at a young age. I helped with daily ch[ores] around the house and helped my mom care for my brother. My m[om] stayed single until she remarried when I was eleven years old. [I] gained another brother and that was the greatest blessing out of [that] relationship. Unfortunately, her new husband would become [yet] another man who would prove to be selfish and emotionally cr[uel.] Once again, we did not have an example of a selfless, loving, [un-] derhearted, kind man that loved God and put others before him[self.]

I knew early on that I needed to help my mom and my two young[er] brothers any way that I could. I didn't always make the right cho[ice] as a child. We would have our days of sibling rivalry, but wh[en] it came down to it, I always protected my brothers and tried to [be] there for them when they needed me.

I also learned life lessons that helped to shape who I am. I cu[lti-] vated a strong work ethic early in life, and I learned how [to] serve with a happy heart (most of the time). We did not al[-] ways have many worldly possessions; in fact, some seasons of [life] we had very little. But we had a royal love. Consider the word[s of] 1 Peter 2:9: "But ye are a chosen generation, a royal priesthoo[d, a] holy nation, a peculiar people; that ye should show forth the pra[is-] es of him who called you out of darkness into his wonderful lig[ht."]

We are special, royal in his light, and chosen. My mother tau[ght] us that no matter our circumstances, this is who we are in Chr[ist.] Needless to say, it makes it so much easier to face the da[rk-] ness and to walk through the trials of this life knowing wh[o] for you, and that there is more than the here and now mome[nt] of this life. Even through generations of mistakes, God gives [us] his overcoming spirit within us that can change the course of [our] lives forever. The truth and light of his word and our choices [are] like the one, two, three punch to the enemy's plans on human[ity.]

Mom remarried for the third time when I was in the eighth gra[de.] We were a blended family of six children. To say it was difficu[lt is] an understatement. There was so much adversity and dysfu[nc-] tion, because once again my mom chose a man like all the m[en] she had ever known, beginning with her father. We had two d[if-] ferent families trying to blend and find unity with so much ang[er] and pain, coupled with the lack of a fatherly example. My m[om] was determined to make it work and bring good out of the situ[a-] tion. She did succeed in bringing one of her stepdaughters to Chr[ist.]

The older I got, the more I realized that this was an area that prov[ed] difficult for my mom, because she never had a good example in [the] life of how a man should treat his wife and children. It was an a[rea] of her heart that wasn't fully healed and whole through Christ. Sh[e] somehow managed to teach us self-worth and value, yet she never fully grabbed a hold of it for herself.

As my frustration and disappointment grew, I just tried to stay away from home with friends as much as I could. I would take on the role of protecting my brothers from the dysfunction as much as I could. Arguing and fighting became a regular occurrence among the younger children and with my stepparent. Even at a young age, I sensed that part of my calling was loving them with all I had and trying to be a good example for them.

Even though we would attend different churches with my mom for some periods of time, it was very difficult to stay plugged in completely due to our family dynamics. Yet all the while, my mom remained committed to always teaching us about Christ and our value in him. We frequently enjoyed long talks and prayed together for God to be the center of our hearts and for us to grow in our relationship with Jesus.

Then, in high school, I met the love of my life, Erik. I knew pretty quickly he would be the man I would marry one day. He respected my values and was one of the most positive, caring guys I had ever met. In our living room, with my mom and I both present, Erik asked Jesus into his heart. That moment set him on the path of knowing Jesus and experiencing Jesus for himself. Erik and my mom often enjoyed long conversations about God and the Bible. Erik had an open heart and felt God's presence in his life. It was beautiful to be a part of watching someone discover freedom and an incredible, miraculous God.

We have been married for nineteen years, and together for twenty-six years. We have definitely had our fair share of ups and downs, but through it all, Erik has always shown amazing caring and devotion for both me and my family. I remember dreaming of the way my husband would be one day, and yes, he filled the tall, dark, and handsome type, but also so much more.

We have withstood our own trials, especially during those early dating years, as we navigated together the issues of trust, loyalty, honesty, and acceptance, even as we worked out our own salvations. But God knew what he was doing, and it has been an endless joy living this life with a man that has a heart for God and his people.

We have two incredible children that amaze us every day! They have such a different life than I had and such grateful and happy hearts. We talk openly about how my husband and I grew up so that they can know and see the difference of a life with two parents and Jesus as the center of one's life. I know that they will have their own struggles, but they will conquer them all because they know their first royal love, Jesus. He makes them whole and complete, no matter their imperfections or challenges.

Knowing your value and worth is irreplaceable. He is a good Father and works all things for our good. It is important to know there is a battle for your heart, and that God created you out of love and for the purpose of sharing his love.

A Royal Love Revealed is about opening our eyes to a love that is unshakable and all consuming. It is a kind of love that brings life to every area of our heart. We need to guard our heart, keeping it safe from things that would darken it or make it fragmented. Jesus came to give us a new heart. Through his Spirit, we have this beautiful gift of joy, peace, and love, whether we are in a valley or on the mountaintop. I'm not talking about a religion. I'm talking about knowing a beautiful, glorious, magnificent, regal-in-stature, pure God who is found in the simple. He gives boundless love. He is always willing to meet you where you are and give you everything you need to get up and walk again with freedom and strength through turning to him. He is a God who is about us having a relationship with him and loving those around us. I wrote this book, but it is God who has unequivocally inspired this book through his messages and through the hearts and whispers to my heart as I sought him through this journey. Death, loss, pain, loneliness, hurt, and sadness can be healed and carried by a loving Father. Remember the words of 2 Corinthians 4:16: "So we do not lose heart. Though our outer self is wasting away, our inner self is renewed day by day." I am just a girl who has experienced God through the trials and victories in my life. This book is all about him and how he loves.

When the veil was torn in two, we became heirs with Christ, a Royal Priesthood. We are a chosen people. I think of Hebrews 10:19 and 1 Peter 2:9–10. The veil was in the temple and only the priests of the time could enter behind it where the presence of God dwelled. This is before Christ came and shed is blood for all to become a royal people who choose to receive Jesus. In doing so, his spirit is alive inside of each of us when we receive him into our hearts. "For you created my inmost being; you knit me together in my mother's womb" (Psalm 139:13).

God gives each of us a passion in our hearts for us to live out, and in doing so, he shows us our first passion, Jesus. How this realization is discovered and comes to pass is through seeking a God that gives us value and purpose. He will speak to your heart and you will have all that you need to fulfill your passion and be made whole in his presence.

My prayer is that the message of this book will draw you closer to a miraculous, available God who desires to lavish his love over you so that your life is established in love, value, and commitment to his ways: a royal love revealed!

When the veil was torn, it became just you and me: that's all, that's everything—heart to heart. Heaven and earth, I am forever yours. You give me life. I think of Psalm 136. God's love never fails. The only time we can use never and always and know it will come to pass is from the living words of an all-knowing God.

CHAPTER 1

─────

ROYAL LOVE
Love As You Have Been Loved

All it takes is an experience with God to show us how available and ready he is to fulfill our every need. Life's storms come—and the world offers temporary reliefs meant to ease our minds—but these storms are not lasting. The only lasting help and hope that grows us to receive more strength, love, peace, and wisdom is our relationship with our Heavenly Father. The one who is Love.

We hold the key to his heart and ours. Real love is a choice. I experienced God beyond words after my mom, Janet Pittman, passed into eternity, but it wasn't just for me. His love is meant to share, so I'm putting my experience into a book. My hope is that it encourages and draws people closer to God, knowing that when we stop and listen, we begin to learn that God is right here with us, wanting to lavish his love over us like a banner! Song of Solomon 2:4 makes clear that the one and most important gaze of the Father for his children is love: "He brought me to the banqueting house, and his banner over me was love."

First, however, we must choose to "put on" love, to adopt a loving attitude. We have our part in royal love. Colossians 3:14 states, "But above all these things put on charity, which is the bond of perfectness." We can think of the word *charity* here as meaning "love for humanity." Love binds us in his perfection.

If we are honest, part of us is restless and always in need of something more. Sometimes we can fill this part for a moment with physical objects, relationships, or busyness, but such distractions do not quench our spiritual needs. Our Heavenly Father completes us in his perfect love. His love brings restoration, comfort, healing, joy, and peace, the kind of love that is not like the world's love, which can be twisted for manipulation or control. God's royal love is the kind of love that is a choice, not just a feeling, created to hold peace as a mantle of our hearts.

My mom loved Jesus's heart and wanted to show his love in tangible ways, big and small. She wore a heart-shaped ring she had a jeweler make years ago, worn as a wedding ring and a representation of Christ's love. She told me that she had it made because it represented our marriage to Christ. We are his bride and he is love.

During the holidays, Mom weaved images of hearts throughout our home and always gave us cards with hand-drawn hearts. She was intentional about serving others less fortunate throughout the year. Mom was wonderful with thinking of ways to show love and with giving God all the credit.

My family has a cherished history with this beautiful symbol, which I look forward to sharing with the reader. I don't share the background of the heart story to say, "Look how special we are." I share it to urge the reader to look back at his or her own life. Consider what might have seemed insignificant or what might have felt like empty pain and realize that God wants to use those things to tell us how much he loves us. Through those experiences, we can be thankful for his blessings.

One afternoon, the first year of Mom's passing, I was picking my daughter up from school, and when she sat in the car, she had a heart drawn on her hand. I questioned her about the heart, and she replied that she thought it was for Sitty, which was what my children called my mother. I asked her, "What do you mean?"

WE HOLD
THE KEY
TO HIS HEART
& OURS.

♥

REAL
LOVE IS
A CHOICE.

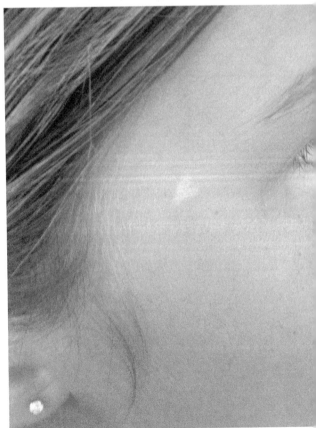

"ARISE, SHINE; FOR THY LIGHT IS COME, AND THE GLORY OF THE LORD IS RISEN UPON THEE."
ISAIAH 60:1

♥

She said, "I told the substitute teacher I have a grandma that is in heaven now. Then, she drew a heart on my hand."

How incredible that God would work through that moment to encourage a child. The substitute teacher had no knowledge of the story. God loves us through our pain, through the good, through everything, and he yearns to be close to us and be our everything!

Later that summer, we went hiking in the Carolina Mountains with family. The kids and I were talking about how Mom would have loved to have been outdoors with us, taking in all of the beauty. She loved the mountains. Later, we were walking on the trails and my sister-in-law noticed that we were surrounded by a vine and that the vine's leaves were heart shaped. We all smiled and thanked God for reminding us of his love and that Mom was with him loving on us. Also, on that hiking vacation, I purchased a heart painting I found in a small art store by a local artist because it reminded me of God's message of love. We thought it amazing that it was the only heart art in the entire store and even that it was there.

When I started sharing my heart encounters with other people, I encouraged them that God could show them hearts or anything else that he spoke to their hearts. My stepsister, Alecia, was very close to my mother, and she would call Mom on a weekly, and sometimes daily, basis to receive any wisdom Mom had to share about life and to be encouraged by their relationship. They would talk frequently about God and growing stronger in their faith. While working through her own grieving process, Alecia walked through a parking lot one day and found a heart-shaped leaf placed directly in front of her feet.

Alecia was thrilled and encouraged by God revealing himself to her in this way.

Time passed and another family vacation came our way. It had been two and a half years since Mom's passing. We were at dinner when my son announced, "I'm looking for a heart, but I don't see one."

I replied, "Well, I don't think there is one, honey. I know you miss Sitty and love seeing the hearts, but I don't see any hearts."

Within minutes, our waitress returned to the table to check on us. My husband exclaimed to my son, "You got your heart!" We marveled that the waitress had two heart patches on her shirt.

When God reveals his love to us, we are called to turn and share it with others. We all received this special love note that evening and couldn't help but share it with others, as to say he loves us all with this passion.

On another occasion, my daughter scratched her face somehow. She couldn't remember what it was from, but as it healed, it turned from a straight line to a heart shape on her face. We are forever marked by his faithfulness and goodness—a witness for others and a reminder of who we belong to. My daughter couldn't believe her eyes! Talk about an outpouring of love for such a small child and for everyone who witnessed this scratch healing as a heart.

Love is embodied clearly in 1 Corinthians 13:4–8: "Charity suffereth long, and is kind; charity envieth not; charity vaunteth not itself, is

not puffed up, / Doth not behave itself unseemly, seeketh not her own, is not easily provoked, thinketh no evil; / Rejoiceth not in iniquity, but rejoiceth in the truth; / Beareth all things, believeth all things, hopeth all things, endureth all things. / Charity never faileth. . . ." Again, we see the word *charity*, which translates into the word love in newer versions of the Bible. This word *charity* made me think how loving our God is in his charity toward us. He showed us these incredible hearts and brought all of us together with his message of grace and steadfast love.

While on spring break, our children took a bike ride to an old fort near where we live. As we walked out on the pier, my husband and I saw a heart in the sky! Proverbs 27:19 explains it so simply yet so profoundly: "As water reflects the face, so one's life reflects the heart." Our everyday choices are a reflection of our heart. Are we loving how we have been loved by Jesus? Do we build up our families with kind, encouraging words? Do we give honor and respect to the people we encounter each day? Do we nurture fruitful bonds that give life and, in return, give us life?

My daughter, Loren, was reminded of this love while eating her breakfast of oatmeal one morning. Matthew 19:14 tells us, "But Jesus said, Suffer little children, and forbid them not, to come unto me: for of such is the kingdom of heaven." Our children can learn at an early age how to see and hear the Lord as they mature. The Lord's voice is the most important voice for them to hear each day, because they are faced daily with the voices and influences in our culture.

Loren came to me one day saying that she thought she saw a heart shape in her bread. I didn't see it and said, "It must be just for you, honey." Later, walking out and then returning through the door to our garage, I looked down and saw this heart on our floor. I exclaimed, "Well, I guess God had something for both of us today, my love!" I tried to wipe the heart to see if it could be washed away, but it couldn't. Five months later, it was gone. As 1 John 3:18–19 instructs us, "My little children, let us not love in word, neither in tongue; but in deed and in truth. / And hereby we know that we are of the truth, and shall assure our hearts before him." Love is an action, not something we merely say. I love this scripture because it really speaks to being genuine and walking out who we are and by *doing*, if we say we are Christ's followers.

In Jesus Culture's song "One Thing Remains," they share that God's love never fails and never gives up on us. His love will never run out on us. If we understood that his love is one that we cannot control or change but that is out of his totally consuming loving nature, I think we would be a lot stronger and joyous in our daily lives. If anything, it is incomprehensible, with our being imperfect and downright selfish, that he gave his life that we might know true love, his love, which is limitless and which hits us at the core of our soul. We know it when we feel because it brings truth, life, love, and an overwhelming feeling of being found and anchored in an everlasting relationship.

LOVE IS THE SINGLE MOST DEFINING QUALITY OF GOD'S CHARACTER AND HIS LIFE. GOD IS A JEALOUS LOVER. OUT OF HIS LOVE, HE CREATES US FOR LOVE.

♥

We were all created in God's image; therefore, we bear his likeness and have the desires of his heart. To love and be loved! God is Love! Without God, there would be no love in the world. It is the source of goodness, as described in 1 Corinthians 13. Truth, justice, mercy, kindness, hope, patience—the whole chapter! And now abide faith, hope, and love, these three; but the greatest of these is love!

This is a war, a war for our hearts. "And we have known and believed the love that God hath to us. God is love; and he that dwelleth in love dwelleth in God, and God in him" (1 John 4:16). Love is the single most defining quality of God's character and his life. God is a jealous lover. Out of his love, he creates us for love.

We are deeply relational because our Creator is relational. When we look at the Trinity, we see an intimate relationship of love. Love and intimacy is the core of his being, and so he gives each of us a heart like his. When God does this, he reveals our deepest purpose: to love and to be loved. Why else would love be the deepest yearning of our hearts? Isn't love one of our greatest joys, and the loss of love our greatest sorrow?

We are again shown how to love through Luke 10:27: "And he answering said, Thou shalt love the Lord thy God with all thy heart, and with all thy soul, and with all thy strength, and with all thy mind, and thy neighbor as thyself." Jeremiah 31:3 proclaims, "The Lord hath appeared of old unto me, saying, Yea, I have loved thee with an everlasting love: therefore with lovingkindness have I drawn thee." Everything hinges on knowing the One who is love. Forever is at stake—a forever of purpose and value beyond our wildest dreams. Life and love forever. Pastor and author of *Crazy Love: Overwhelmed by a Relentless God*, Francis Chan has made a profound statement based on scripture as to what is most important to God for his people: how we love others is how God will measure our lives. For us to believe in Jesus is to see when he moves in our lives. We were on a family vacation and my son was resting in the hotel room.

YOUR LOVE IS ROYAL, LORD. YOU ARE THE ONE TRUE KING WHO RULES OVER THE UNIVERSE WITH PURE LOVE.

♥

He looked up and, clear as day, said, "Look what's on the door, Mom." I looked and couldn't believe that I was seeing, a heart shape design in the wood door. Instantly, I thought of the word *hope*. John 3:16 tells us that "For God so loved the world, that he gave his only begotten Son, that whosoever believeth in him should not perish, but have everlasting life."

Your love is royal, Lord. You are the one true King who rules over the universe with pure love. Regal in stature truth, justice, mercy, and pureness are yours. You are the author and finisher of our faith.

My niece Blake saw this heart shape after water spilled on the floor, while visiting my brother. Blake was reunited with her mother after a difficult divorce. Coping with loss and pain, she has questioned herself and life's challenges. God cares for all our struggles, and he has proven himself loving and present through the heart sightings to Blake. Psalm

91:14 proclaims, "Because he has set his love upon me, therefore I ᵕ deliver him; I will set him on high, because he has known my nar Blake has been delivered from her past circumstances and exp enced a great love in rebuilding her relationship with her mom, she has continually grown stronger in her new relationship with Je

Just days before my husband was set to leave for his mission to Haiti and a week exactly to the day before my mom's birth God had something to say. My daughter took a sip of water one drop fell on her shirt. Plumb's song "One Drop" immedia came to mind, reminding me that it only takes one drop of Go love and our total commitment to our dreams to change the wo Psalm 91:1–2 teaches, "He that dwelleth in the secret place of Most High shall abide under the shadow of the Almighty. / I will of the Lord, He is my refuge and my fortress: my God; in him w

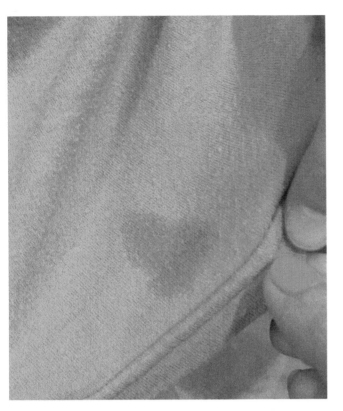

GOD'S ROYAL LOVE FILLS US WITH LOVE, AND THEN WE FILL OTHERS BY SHARING THIS LOVE.

♥

trust." To *dwell* means "to live or stay as a permanent resident" and "to live or continue in a given condition." Abiding under his shadow means to have the benefits of his covering and protection because we have positioned ourselves according to his ways to receive from him. The verse also states that he is our refuge and fortress. *Refuge* is defined by a "condition of being safe or sheltered from pursuit, danger, or trouble." Now what pursuit or danger would possibly be a threat to us? There is one who desires to see us fall and be destroyed. John 10:10 explains, "The thief cometh not, but for to steal, and to kill, and to destroy: I am come that they might have life, and that they might have it more abundantly." The thief is Satan. He brings destruction and death to a fallen world, not the one who is love, God our Father. This heart photo, taken on the Inca Trail in Peru, came from a dear friend who lives this scripture so well. Mark 12:30–31 commands us to love: "And thou shalt love the Lord thy God with all they heart,

and with all thy mind, and with all thy strength: this is the first commandment. / And the second is like, namely this, Thou shalt love thy neighbor as thyself. There is none other commandment greater than these." We are asked to love the Father with all our hearts and to love others as ourselves. Once again, we are called to a higher way of life. God's royal love fills us with love, and then we fill others by sharing this love. We are here to show love as we have been loved. Toward the end of this awesome scripture, we are returned to the truth that nothing greater exists. There is nothing greater than love, the love we share that has been shared with us by God.

CHAPTER 1

———

HEART BEATS

♥ one.

How would our lives be measured through the way we love?
Consider performing random acts of kindness through the giving
of time, treasure, or talent, with no expectations in return.

♥ two.

How could you love those closest to you in deed and not just words?
Invite them over to dinner every few weeks or write them
a heartfelt message.

WHAT IS GOD SAYING TO ME TODAY?

CHAPTER 2

—

PRIDE
A Spiritual Cancer

Even in saying yes to God, raising up the foundations of generations can still be messy. I see this journey of life as stepping stones, dependent upon how obedient and willing we are to let problems and control go and to have open hearts before the one who made our hearts. As we do so, we continue to step in sync with his plan.

We can be tempted to let bitterness, pride, unforgiveness, and shame block us; these emotions build walls around us. We may try to fix and hide our emotions in our own efforts to avoid or wall ourselves from others, to create our own safe zone, but these efforts fail us. Hebrews 12:15 warns us against such emotions: "Looking carefully lest anyone fall short of the grace of God; lest any root of bitterness springing up cause trouble; and by th is many become defiled."

We all have, though, our defense mechanisms. Once we learn who's we are and who is against us, it helps us to see more clearly and to live life with an open hand, not internalizing others' shortcomings or thinking that we cannot move beyond our own. We all have imperfections! Humility is pride's antidote. Jesus gave us the example of true humility so that we can know how to overcome the entanglement and isolation of pride.

"Wisdom is the principal thing; therefore get wisdom and with all they getting get understanding. / Exalt her, and she shall promote thee: she bring thee to honour, when thou dost embrace her. / She shall give to thine head an ornament of grace: a crown of glory shall she deliver to thee." Proverbs 4:7–9

Wisdom gets you there. If you don't have the wisdom and knowledge to stand and navigate through life's daily battles for your heart, you have no weapon. Our enemies aren't each other, although the w tells us so. They are spiritual principalities and the things unsee this world. Our enemy is not in the flesh but in spirit. God wants eryone to come into a relationship with him and receive eternity, we do have an adversary who wants the opposite and does everyth he can to stop God's redemptive work. Our lives are about restora and God's love making us whole.

Remember that the war is for our hearts. I am reminded of (City's song "You're Not Alone" that assures us we are in a relations with Jesus. It is comforting to know that we are not alone and this real, alive, loving, and personal Jesus never turns away from and keeps us until we are in his arms again. Ephesians 3:13–19 co pels us to connect with God: "Wherefore I desire that ye faint no my tribulations for you, which is your glory. / For this cause I bow knees unto the Father of our Lord Jesus Christ, / Of whom the wh family in heaven and earth is named, / That he would grant you, cording to the riches of his glory, to be straightened with migh his Spirit in the inner man; / That Christ may dwell in your he by faith; that ye, being rooted and grounded in love, / May be to comprehend with all saints what is the breadth, and length, depth, and height; / And to know the love of Christ, which pass knowledge, that ye might be filled with all the fulness of God." Pr among other shortcomings, blocks that connection.

WE CAN BE
TEMPTED TO LET
BITTERNESS,
PRIDE,
UNFORGIVENESS,
& SHAME
BLOCK US;
THESE EMOTIONS
BUILD WALLS
AROUND US.

♥

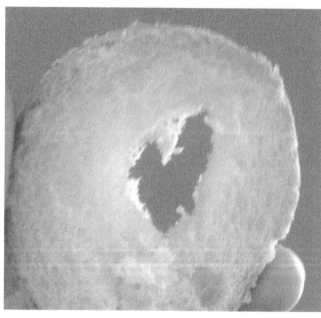

While cleaning the house one day, I cleaned a mirror. Later, getting dressed, I noticed a tiny image on the mirror. I looked closer and couldn't believe what I saw. It was a heart. The British novelist, poet, and essayist C.S. Lewis has written so well that contentment, even a chance of love or common sense, is not possible, because of the spiritual cancer of pride. I can think of so many experiences in my life where the result of pride was senseless, devastating, and counterproductive. I have learned that pride gives us a false sense of control and builds walls that darken our ability to love freely. Our hearts start to grow a hard shell in pride, but humility softens them with peace, love, and joy.

We have an enemy, the same enemy who deceived Adam and Eve in the Garden of Eden. When he comes to kill, steal, and destroy, it's not always in one blow; it's often over time, trying to gradually chip away at our hearts—to fracture and divide them. The oldest trick in the book is to divide and conquer. Revelations 12:10 tells us, "And I heard a loud voice saying in heaven, Now is come salvation, and strength, and the kingdom of our God, and the power of his Christ: for the accuser of our brethren is cast down, which accused them before our God day and night." We hear other voices in our heads, besides our own, that try to keep us from living free from condemnation. The only weapon the enemy has is thoughts and suggestions that are not our reality.

hough the enemy would have us believe otherwise, we are encour-
d in John 10:10 that our lives can have abundance: "I am come
t they might have life, and that they might have it more abundant-
Pride, and other spiritual cancers, robs us of that abundant life.

husband had an interview for some work that he really would
e loved. It would have been a great opportunity for his company.
ore walking into the interview, he saw a heart sticker on the door.
thought it was incredible and texted a photo to me. Many months
r, while writing this book, my husband was awarded two incred-
job opportunities with this wonderful organization that we know
love as the University of Florida. God is our provider.

most one year later, while walking off the UF football field after
husband and his team were honored for completing an indoor
tball practice facility for the university, a large drop of water in the
pe of a heart was in my path. Water had dripped from above to
lower ramp in the stadium. God is faithful to complete and can
omplish more than we can ever imagine, if we don't strive in pride
rely on Jesus and trust him as we do the works he has called us
do.

ter that same day, my sweet mother-in-law prepared a birthday
ner to celebrate. My daughter took a bite out of her bread and
amazing heart space was left in it. He is the Great I Am!

another occasion, we were at the beach looking for sharks' teeth,
we found heart-shaped shells right in front of us. My daughter
nd the larger black shell, and I found the other two. Romans
0 reminds us, "For the invisible things of him from the creation
the world are clearly seen, being understood by things that are
de, even his eternal power and Godhead; so that they are without
use." We are called to lay our pride down so that we can receive

God's eternal power. He is the only one who truly holds all power
and who knows what is best for our humanity.

We were at the beach gathering shells and found heart-shaped
shells before us, so clear. We praise the Lord of Lords forever. He is
the author of the unexplainable. Romans 12:9 commands us, "Let
love be without dissimulation. Abhor that which is evil; cleave to
that which is good." Love must be sincere. This is so profound. To
be sincere is to be "free from pretense or deceit" or "proceeding from
genuine feelings." God is telling us the attributes of love and to
what we should cling. Pride is the opposite of these attributes. If our
own satisfaction only comes from our personal achievements, that
satisfaction is based on pretentiousness and is not sincere. Remember true contentment and peace is apart from deceit. We don't want
to will those things in our lives through pride but to find God's will
through his nature and enjoy all of the benefits of being in a royal
family where everything is already in order. All that is required is
our loyalty.

How do your actions affect someone else when you're focused only on
yourself? As children of God, we don't have to strive as man strives.
As we abide in him, pride has no place and our trust is established in
him. We are humbled because we experience an eternal God who is
alive and active in our lives. Our relationship with him grows and he
is made bigger in our hearts. In Christ, we have favor, and he moves
all things for our good and provision, trusting in his word and ways.
Hebrews 6:19 shows us the eternal hope available to us: "Which
hope we have as an anchor for the soul, both sure and steadfast, and
which entereth into that within the vail." The vail in this scripture
refers to being in the inner sanctuary of God's presence. His truths
are revealed to us—not to special people, but to anyone who seeks
him and has a pure heart before him.

GOD'S ROYAL LOVE IS ALL AROUND US. HE SEES IT ALL AND SAYS, "I LOVE YOU AND I AM HERE. I'LL NEVER LEAVE."

♥

Your value comes from the creator, from what his word says. It does not come from what others say or think. Others do not give us our value. Compliments are nice but not what we hang our self-worth on. Knowing and experiencing him gives us everything we need. Loving others with sincerity is what we are called to do as the body of Christ. Grace encourages us to pick up again and do it better. When we don't extend grace that is where the enemy can come in and devastate relationships with everyone we know.

The enemy wants isolation and missed opportunities of learning from a brother or sister in Christ. Pride is a stone wall; it puffs up against anything that doesn't come from itself. It creates a false image of self-protection. When in fact, the only thing we are preserving is our ego. James 4:6 points out who receives grace: "But he giveth more grace. Wherefore he saith, God resisteth the proud, but giveth grace unto the humble."

Psalms 37:11 states, "But the meek shall inherit the earth; and shall delight themselves in abundance of peace." In Christ, we are free to be real and to share the realities of our world, but with humbleness, knowing that in love, condemnation is absent; grace remains. As children of God, we have grace that says, "I still love you, but get up and do it the right way now." When we release pride, we always learn something new. Moreover, when we confess our sins, we are made new.

We believe that a loving Father who wants us complete in him is molding us all the time. We never stop learning from the one who holds all knowledge and wisdom. He shares it with us, but he is the source of it all, endlessly. Deuteronomy 7:9 declares, "Know therefore that the Lord thy God, he is God, the faithful God, which keepeth covenant and mercy with them that love him and keep his commandments to a thousand generations." If you love someone, you want to please them and show in return your devotion, not seek your own selfish desires.

In 1 John 2:3–4 we come to know our Lord in a special way: "_ hereby we do know that we know him, if we keep his comma ments. / He that saith, I know him, and kept not his commandme is a liar, and the truth is not in him." Like the commandments, hearts in this book are a beautiful representation of his grace, hope, comfort, healing, embrace, and steadfast presence, if we open our hearts and eyes to see him in his splendid glory. Our can only be open through humility—not through pride in our knowledge.

The peace of God comes from being with him. We can't have p within ourselves if we are not in a posture of humility to receive f the one who is all knowing. Colossians 3:15 proclaims, "And let peace of God rule in your hearts, to the which also ye are called in body; and be ye thankful." As I was taking care of my mom, I ha lay down my own desires and serve humbly. I had to create spac my life to hear from God. Most important, I had to stay in a pos of receiving from Jesus to give me peace and direction each da caring for my mom and my family. I can honestly say that the sm I became, the more able I was to give. Each day, even if it was a l chaotic at times, was filled with intentionality and grace. Hone after Mom went into eternity, I grew in my reverence for God. I grown a better understanding of God's ways, which are higher different from our own, and it is OK to have rest in his answer.

God's royal love is all around us. He sees it all and says, "I love and I am here. I'll never leave." God says, "Turn back to me, and give you everything you need." Acts 3:19 call us to "Repent, ye th fore, and be converted, that your sins may be blotted out, when times of refreshing shall come from the presence of the Lord." It i the repenting or confessing that we release our sins, and then in turning, he meets us and takes it all and, furthermore, refreshes We also lay down our pride in this posture of openness and willi ness. We don't have to defend. He is our defender! We lack noth because of him who is in us. The complete fullness in his presenc the unexplainable! It brings joy to my heart to know this God enjoy the benefits of his perfection.

The world says to hide our physical and emotional flaws. Christ says, though, to bring them into his light and let him bring his goodness through them. He is shown bigger and faithful as a perfect Father. To know our savior is to know how great and glorious he is. It is through him we are made strong. God sees from the inside out. Matthew 23:25–26 reveals Christ's message to the scribes and Pharisees: "Woe unto you, scribes and Pharisees, hypocrites! For ye make clean the outside of the cup and of the platter, but within they are full of extortion and excess. / Thou blind Pharisee, cleanse first that which is within the cup and platter, that the outside of them may be clean also." It's quite the opposite of the world system. We are implored to clean from within our hearts, and then our outer man will be cleansed as well. God is more concerned with the health of our hearts. As Christians, we need not to judge but to love. This is a work in progress for most of us, me included.

My husband, Erik, knows all too well the inclination to "make things happen" being in the construction industry. He has discovered that releasing it all to God frees him to be all God has called him to be for others. Everything else God works out for the good and to benefit people and his plans. It frees Erik up to be a light within his social and business circles each day. On one particular day, he sat outside with me sharing that his time at work was about to get busier and talking through the challenges and concerns as to how to handle it all effectively. He prayed and then looked down to see that a drop of water on his chair had made a heart shape. Seek him first in all things big and small.

Two days after my son's birthday, I encountered another heart in the last bite of my spaghetti. It was good, and I was scraping the bowl, when I noticed the heart-shaped bit on my fork. Psalm 34:8 proclaims, "O taste and see that the Lord is good; blessed is the man that trusteth in him." When we trust and take refuge in him, releasing pride, we are blessed.

I like sharing the definitions of some of the words in scripture because I think it helps us to understand fully the meaning in God's word. Sometimes we misuse words out of habit. *Blessed* is defined as "made holy" and "consecrated." We can be made holy or have any of Christ's attributes only if we take refuge in him, if we let ourselves be consumed by his presence of love and beauty, made possible when we give up pride. Letting go of pride let me see God around me. Erik received a special blessing that evening, knowing that he does not have all the answers, as he sought God for direction and humbled himself to hear from our all-knowing God.

CHAPTER 2

———

HEART BEATS

♥ one.

What areas do we protect because we are afraid of shame and rejection?
Say a simple daily prayer, then listen: Jesus, show me the areas I protect
and guard. Holy Spirit, shine your love on those areas of brokenness
and remind me that no one is perfect and that we are complete only in
Christ.

♥ two.

How do we effectively serve others when we don't feel like it, or when
we feel like it is too much to give or accomplish? Begin with asking
yourself, what is it that God is asking you to do? Then proceed to do it
in a manner of trusting Jesus and knowing that he will make the way
clear for you and help you to see it to completion.

WHAT IS GOD SAYING TO ME TODAY?

CHAPTER 3

____

BREATHE
Under His Wing

Many times while caring for Mom, I felt my breath taken from me briefly while witnessing her pain and circumstances. God showed me where we could help Mom and where we could be his refreshing breath she needed. She had those moments with him herself, but he calls his church to be a part of all he does. We, in relationship with each other, compel one another onward to this higher call of sacrificial love. Jesus came to say that he is life and he can breathe life into all things and use it to point people to his heart.

On August 6, 2011, I was sitting on the couch watching the kids play and happened to look up at the plant a sweet couple at my church had given my mom when she came home from the hospital. They were the same couple who'd prayed with Mom when she received the news about her diagnoses of colon cancer. The leaves on the plant were in the perfect shape of a heart! I could not contain myself. The kids and I were in complete awe. God is so faithful! Isaiah 52:12 encourages us that we are not alone: "For ye shall not go out with haste, nor go by flight: for the Lord will go before you; and the God of Israel will be your rearward." The scripture comforts us in knowing that we need never fear what is ahead, for God goes before us, is with us, and is our rear guard!

Prior to the school year starting, we took a weekend trip to a hotel that had a lazy river swimming pool. While we floated in our rafts, the kids shared about how much they missed Sitty and how much they wished she could be with us on vacation. My mom would go on our family vacations with us from time to time to get away and enjoy life with us. She could not afford her own vacation time. My husband glanced over at the side of the pool while trying to get a raft and said, "You're not going to believe this! There's a heart etched out in the concrete on the side of the pool!"

"HE RESTORETH MY SOUL: HE LEADETH ME IN THE PATH OF RIGHTEOUSNESS FOR HIS NAME'S SAKE."
PSALM 23:3

We both said to the kids, "Sitty and God are here with us," then I added, "God is so incredible!" We didn't have a camera and it was on the inside of the lazy river track, so I could get a photograph. It didn't stop there, though. When we turned to our room, my daughter grabbed a snack of pretzels and pulled a heart-shaped pretzel out of the bag just for

Many heart moments have been in my own home. My sister-in-law Cheryl was relaxing at my house for Sunday dinner noticed my lights that hang in the center of my home have heart shapes on every side when looking up at them from sitting on sofa. I'm reminded of James 1:2–3: "My brethren, count it all when you fall into divers temptations; / Knowing this, that trying of your faith worketh patience." This scripture explains to when we fall into troubles, let it be an opportunity for joy. Because when our faith is tested, our endurance has a chance to grow. Like a runner, endurance comes from being tested in speed or distance; the runner must learn to control breathing. Holding

breath or breathing too fast can make this process harder. When your breath is in step, your body is calm and relaxed. Like running and our testing of faith, when our endurance is fully developed, we will be ready for that run and strong through our steadfast faith. During a trip to the beach, we looked for sharks' teeth, and I found these two shells broken into a heart shape! The experience reminded me of Luke 12:34: "For where your treasure is, there will your heart be also."

A week later, toward the end of the summer, I returned to the same beach location with my mom's dearest friend, Christine. She was feeling heavyhearted, remembering Mom and watching my children play, feeling a deep compassion for what we have endured together as a family in not having Mom with us anymore. Christine said to me, "I've been thinking about your mom, and I just am missing her and am thankful for us remaining friends." Then, looking down the beach and into the sky, she said, "Do you see the hearts?"

I looked and said, "No, I don't see it."

Joking, Christine said, "Girl, you better get your heart eyes on."

A short time later, while looking for sharks' teeth, I noticed a dark-colored shell, a perfect heart shape broken out. I picked it up thinking that out of this entire beach, I had walked up and found there in my path this fantastic gift, and I wasn't even looking for it. Amazing! Our God is full of all the wonder, so great we can't even imagine. Hebrews 4:9–11 reminds us, "There remaineth therefore a rest to the people of God. / For he that is entered into his rest, he also hath ceased from his own works, as God did from his. / Let us labour therefore to enter into that rest, lest any man fall after the same example of unbelief." As this scripture says, we can fully rest in the presence of God. Yielding ourselves to his power and strength keeps us from falling into disobedience. We put our own works in check with what works God calls us to complete first.

The day before my birthday dinner with family, my sister-in-law went to the beach and took a picture of the sky because the clouds looked interesting. When she returned home, she saw what was in the center of the clouds for the first time! The other photo is a shell she found with a heart in it. The red shells were ones we would collect frequently, and I would share them with my mom. I thought of Psalm 91:4: "He shall cover thee with his feathers, and under his wings shalt thou trust: his truth shall be thy shield and buckler." His truth will protect and rescue us. His wings shield us, and his feathers give us shelter. His faithful promises are our armor and protection. When we feel protected and equipped for life's trials, we can breathe again and not feel trapped in despair.

My daughter, Loren, took a sand sifter to the beach with friends on Labor Day and the sand. I thought of Proverbs 17:17: "A friend loveth at all times. . . ." Also, Luke 6:31 came to mind: "And as ye would that men should do to you, do ye also to them likewise." The Holy Spirit spoke to my heart about friendships and the ways God uses them in our lives to strengthen us and to show us God's love to one another.

When we are hit with a negative phone call or a trespass of our hearts, God is there. Immediately, our enemy goes to work speaking lies. He will do anything to shift our gaze from our loving, all-knowing, powerful Father. He speaks smallness, sickness, death, insecurities, accusations, and hopelessness. He tries to take away our breath, to send us into a tailspin of confusion and uncertainty.

I felt this many times while caring for my mom, when facing the harsh realities of lack of provision and sacrifice from her spouse and when seeing her broken heart. This kind of deception tried to choke out our peace and made me feel as if I couldn't breathe. This sort of pain takes our breath away for the moment. We are left with short, shallow gasps of air. We feel our stomachs tighten.

IN GOD'S PRESENCE, WE WALK AWAY FILLED, FULL, AND DRIPPING WITH HIS ENDLESS LOVE AND GRACE.

♥

This kind of darkness makes me feel nauseated. It is a feeling I have only felt at times of great sorrow and when much is at stake. The body responds to these emotions and spiritual despair. We are made for goodness and joy. Quickly, in these moments, I run to the voice of truth and to what my God says about the enemy's lies. My heart runs to stand on the joy that the Lord gives bountifully and to meet him there in his mighty presence. He lifts our cares and worries into his vast arms, and we are covered under his wing. Here is where he speaks truth, love, hope, purpose, and life. Here is where he lights the path of endurance and strength. We are found in his presence and confirmed for his great works. Psalm 119:1–2 reminds us, "Blessed are the undefiled in the way, who walk in the law of the Lord. / Blessed are they that keep his testimonies, and that seek him with the whole heart."

Health scares are certainly moments that can steal away our breath. I had a phone call while on vacation that I had to come back for a second mammogram when a doctor saw something suspicious that hadn't been there previously. I have had regular mammograms since Mom's passing. The first voice that spoke to me was the voice of truth. He said, "This is just a cyst. It is nothing." Over the preceding days, however, until I could get my follow-up appointment, the enemy started with some of those little comments mentioned above. Ever so softly, but ever so consistently. The word, which is him, offered joy as I prayed it over my situation.

As I walked into my appointment, my brother sent me a picture of a heart in the sky over the waters of the ocean with beams of light bursting through. I was so moved by God's reminder of his love and presence—sent right then, at that very moment. His timing is always perfect. I thanked my brother for being God's messenger to me th day. If we have eyes to see and are obedient in doing what God as of us, he does a mighty work through us all. No matter how mu darkness surrounds us, his light shines through and gives us ho and a future. Psalm 27:5 shows us how to rely on him in moments difficulty: "For in the time of trouble he shall hide me in his pavilio in the secret of his tabernacle shall he hide me; he shall set me upon a rock."

In God's presence, we walk away filled full and dripping with his en less love and grace. Nothing compares to these moments when G shows himself true. Don't ever think your moments with Jesus are accident. His love is alive and intentional. You can be in the preser of kings and the world's most influential people, but you will ne leave their presence feeling the way you do after being with the c true King who lives and loves like no one else. Love is war—Go war for the hearts of man and wholeness in him until he retur

The lyrics to the song "Love is War" by Hillsong United sing so w of our sin becoming his own and turning from our own pride i his love. The song goes on to sing that we will fight for love and through our life into the triumph of the Son. His love embraces a completes our hearts when we fully give our hearts to him. There can breathe again with no restriction. We are reminded who fig for us. Romans 15:13 tells us, "Now the God of hope fill you with joy and peace in believing, that ye may abound in hope, through power of the Holy Spirit."

———

HEART BEATS

♥ one.

It is Jesus's breath that breathes life into our difficult circumstances. Enter into his presence through worship, reading scripture, and prayer to be revived and renewed each day.

♥ two.

Jesus gives us lasting peace and confidence in our relationship with him. His word is alive and extends life to our every need. Take time today to write down scriptures that strengthen you, give you peace, and restore your breath through each difficulty.

WHAT IS GOD SAYING TO ME TODAY?

CHAPTER 4

———

CULTIVATING FAITH
Trusting in Him

As I put my daughter to bed one night and we said our prayers, she expressed how much she missed Sitty. I said, "Well, when we pray, let's tell God how much we miss Sitty and ask him to tell her that we love her and miss her." So, we did.

The next day, while traveling to south Florida, my sister-in-law Cheryl called me to say that she had the craziest dream and that she had to tell me. I sat there in amazement about what she shared!

She said that she'd dreamed about Mom. In the dream, Mom was dying. Cheryl was trying to help Mom find something in her room. Mom said, "Go and ask Corrine. She will know where it is." My sister-in-law found the item, and on her way out the door, my mom said, "Tell Corrine I love her." Cheryl said okay, and my mom repeated, "No, tell Corrine that I love her." She was emphasizing her gratitude and love for us caring for her in our home.

I just wept. I was so moved, and I told my sister-in-law what my daughter and I had prayed the night before. We asked God to tell Mom that we loved her and missed her. I joyfully shared it with my daughter, as well. Not only was Mom saying that she loved us, too, but she was also sharing her gratitude for us having her in our home and caring for her for the last months of her life. It still moves me to tears. It brings me to my knees at the reality of how gracious and glorious our God is!

As we continued on our trip down the interstate. I looked out the window. There was a white heart spray-painted on pine trees every few trees for about two miles down the road. Sadly, none of my pictures turned out. We could do nothing but praise God! When has God laid on your heart to call a friend, make a meal for someone, buy someone's lunch, or give someone money? God knows the purpose. We just have to do what he asks us to do. Faith is trusting and doing.

While serving with an outreach program in an impoverished are my city, I decided that I would share the heart story for the first tim young ladies from the neighborhood. I felt called to share how m God loves them. The session ended, and I went outside, where ano woman came up to me and showed me a heart spray-painted on sidewalk. One of the girls helping me in the session that night was w ing big heart earrings. God is always weaving his message and tou ing the hearts of people who are willing to see him. He is everywh

No matter if we are in the valley, hiking up the trails, or on mountaintop, God is with us and moves everything for our goo that we can continue to grow and learn to be more like him. were created in his image and made for the purposes he put motion when he created us. Faith is trusting in him and his poses. We cultivate it by being intentional and stepping out in w he asks us to do. I was unsure about sharing the testimony of hearts, unsure how others would receive it. Through my obedie and willingness to prepare sharing, though, God did someth awesome for someone else. He revealed himself to her and oth

We are the church, the Holy Spirit in us. God wants his peo to bring his love to this earth. It is through listening to his rection and then doing it in faith that we grow. In Hebr 8, God tells us that he will put his laws into our minds by Holy Spirit and write them on our hearts. The word lives breathes in us so that, because of the Holy Spirit, we are emp ered to obey it and complete every work he calls us to compl

HE WORKS ALL THINGS FOR OUR GOOD WHILE WE HAVE COMPLETE TRUST IN HIM, TAKING EACH STEP WITHOUT SEEING THE END.

♥

My son, Hayden, shared with my husband and me that he wanted to purchase some pink sweat wristbands for his next football game in honor of Sitty for National Breast Cancer Awareness Month. Before the next game, he finished eating his lunch and a tiny piece of turkey in the shape of a heart was left on his plate. As he wrapped his jammed finger before his game, he saw a piece of heart-shaped string on the tape. Talk about letting Hayden know that God and Sitty were aware of how he wanted to honor his grandmother and how much he is loved! How different would the world be if more of us stopped each day and made a point to think about how we can honor someone and show our love?

I feel that God is encouraging not only me, but also all those around me through this testimony of the hearts. My hope is that my testimony will help lead others who read this book to look up above their circumstances of this world and seek a relationship with their Creator. I pray that we might experience his love and grace in our lives and that everything we need be added to us to help us have whole hearts and love overflowing during our earthly time.

Our thought life has so much to do with experiencing God for who he is and being able to see him working around and through us. Our minds show us the condition of our hearts, because what we think about, we say and then act upon. Negative or destructive thoughts come to us all. When we pause, make time to read the word, and seek God—even for ten minutes—it helps us to identify our thoughts and decipher which ones are out of the will of God. This enables us to examine better how our thoughts and decisions line up with God's nature and what he is speaking to our hearts.

As my mom used to say, "What goes in must come out." It is so important to guard our hearts and not allow the endless, empty things of this world to shadow the voice of the one who gives us freedom and purpose. Honing your heart to the Lord's takes intentionality in pursuing an endless God! How might the Father speak to you? It could be hearts or it could be something different. All Glory and Honor to the one who gives perfect love and life forever!

Revelation 12:11 points out how we overcome: "And they overcame him by the blood of the Lamb, and by the word of their testimony; and they loved not their lives unto the death." In this scripture, "him" refers to Satan, and we can overcome him because of what Jesus did on the cross. We cultivate our faith by following Jesus's word and learning through our testimonies that he can be trusted to deliver us.

Our reality is not God's reality. He already has the eternity focus which one day we will have, too, because we will be with him. What, though, of now, knowing that this world and time will pass forever? What impact will we make on it for eternity? For the hearts of man. Matthew 7:7 promises that God will be there for us: "Ask, and it shall be given to you; seek, and ye shall find; knock, and it shall be opened unto you." God responds! It's not in one or two knocks. It is in the repetition and constant focus on him who is enough.

That is where he is working in us and molding our hearts and souls to be closer and whole in him. He loves us and wants us to know him. We mold our hearts in the valleys when we are focused on God. When all we have is he, that's when we are transcended into his presence and have eyes fixed on his kingdom and ways. It's the unexplainable mysteries God reveals to us in that time. He is in the unexplainable and miraculous. He works all things for our good while we have complete trust in him, taking each step without seeing the end.

"Lo children are an heritage from the Lord: and the fruit of the womb is his reward. / As arrows are in the hand of a mighty man; so are the children of the youth. / Happy is the man that hath his quiver full of them: they shall not be ashamed, but they shall speak with the enemies in the gate." Psalm 127:3–5

I came home one afternoon to find a heart token on top of our outside trashcan that had been returned up to our garage after trash pickup day. I asked everyone I knew who had put it there, only to discover no one had. I still do not know who left it there, and I believe that they have no knowledge of the heart story. God is with us. He is our strength and refuge.

JESUS STIRS OUR HEARTS AND BRINGS LIVING WATERS TO EVERY AREA OF OUR FRAGMENTED HEARTS.

♥

My friend is writing a book about the personal testimonies of women whom she has met at our church. She sent me a photo of a leaf lying on ivy after seeing it on her morning walk. We had been encouraging and praying for one another while writing our own books, both first-time authors. God will send those around you to encourage you in what he calls you to do. They could be very close friends or someone with whom you have a common purpose. I am thankful that I opened myself up to receive from others with pure motives and to learn from them while pushing each other on in our faith and purpose.

While writing this chapter, the thought came to mind, *what you cultivate will grow.* The word *cultivate* means to "care for." What do we take care of in our lives? Just like a garden, what we care for in the garden will grow and we will have a product at the end. We can have a dry, lifeless garden or a lush, growing, bountiful one. What should we be taking care of in our lives? Are we cultivating our faith? Are we a part of the process in doing things in faith? Are we building our faith by reading and listening to the word of God? The only lasting thing we leave behind in this world is our legacy. What kind of legacy trail will there be for the ones coming behind us?

God is clear in his scripture that this life isn't for our endless consum­tion of selfish desires but for loving others and helping others find th­ way to the one with a royal, wild love. Jesus stirs our hearts and bri­ living waters to every area of our fragmented hearts. He multiples ­ goodness through our active, caring hands and feet. This active fa­ leaves a trail, a trail for others to witness God's character and attribut­

I am reminded of an old saying: "Children learn by what you ­ not by what you say." What you do is a reflection of your heart a­ soul. We can know how to cultivate love in our lives from Ephesia­ 5:2: "And walk in love, as Christ also hath loved us, and hath giv­ himself for us an offering and a sacrifice to God for a sweetsmelli­ savour." In this scripture, the sweet-smelling aroma is referring t­ Corinthians 14, and through us the manifest fragrance of his know­ edge in every place. His knowledge is all around us and strengthe­ us to be active in building his kingdom, which is through faith. H­ reverential that we get to be a part of Jesus's work on the earth a­ that he calls each of us to share his knowledge out of his royal love­

———

HEART BEATS

♥ one.

Self-reflection is critical on our walk with God. Light a candle, sit in silence, and lean into the moment, in order to listen for God to reveal areas of your heart that need strengthening.

♥ two.

We are continually transformed and confirmed as we participate in our faith walk: through the stretching of doing a church outreach, singing in a worship band, writing a book, or being that trusted friend who doesn't judge but, instead, encourages.

WHAT IS GOD SAYING TO ME TODAY?

CHAPTER 5

HUMILITY
Before Honor

We can all agree that this world is hard and so many distractions vie for our time, such as chasing material objects, climbing the corporate ladder, indulging in worldly pleasures, and escaping to our comfort zones. We quickly find ourselves, however, bored and empty, thinking about how fast times passes and what is to come after this world. If this life is so brief, what is after this life? I really let this thought settle with me in a deeper way as I took care of my mom through her struggle with cancer. The Holy Spirit would remind me consistently of Proverbs 15:33: "The fear of the Lord is the instruction of wisdom; and before honor is humility."

When we are obedient in our assignments from God, no matter how difficult or selfless, God honors those who are faithful in his perfect timing. He knows the full work in everyone's hearts. He knows when that work is complete for each moment in time. Our obedience is noble and worthy in his sight. We are set apart for his good works. We are forever changed when we see his plans come to pass. We get the bigger picture that it's not just about ourselves individually, but it's about us collectively. It's about all of humanity coming together, showing God's love, and meeting everyone's needs through his tender love.

I was blessed to be a part of a group of ladies performing an outreach in our community when a special heart moment happened. We had gathered at my house to pray for one another and our outreach one evening. As we were praying, one of the ladies, knowing the story of the hearts, said, "Look, there's a heart shape in your rug. Wait, there's two heart shapes in the rug." Praise God so incredible when he reveals himself as he chooses!

On another occasion, during an important day where I was trusting God for something in my life, I found my prayers were answered. While walking in a parking lot, I looked down and saw a piece of paper in the shape of a heart on the road. When we humble in the waiting and surrendered to him through our vice, God is so faithful. He wants us to know he is with u ways. Proverbs 23:19 reminds us to keep a humble heart: "thou, my son, and be wise, and guide thine heart in the w

A week before Mom's birthday, we were outside and a heart-shaped leaf was before us on the driveway. Our family had been talking a her and ways to remember her and celebrate her birthday. Mom l Steak 'n Shake milk shakes, so we decided that we would par in the creamy treat, making it a tradition and a sweet way for family to honor her memory. Deuteronomy 30:20 reminds u life's key: we can make this choice by loving our God, obeying and committing ourselves firmly to him; this is the key to our l This is a choice, and we need his wisdom to make the best cho

A week prior to starting a period of fasting, we had come h from Sunday church services where we had sought God's w on what he would like us to believe in his provision for and w breakthrough in our lives we should pray for during the fast. W we got home, a heart-shaped leaf was on our doorstep inside garage! No other leaves anywhere. Psalm 5:12 shows us, thou, Lord, wilt bless the righteous; with favour wilt thou c pass him as with a shield.'" His relentless shield of love protect

We should not be distracted by timelines or the world's expe tions planted within us, but we should walk in the way of our sp growing in love and giving love. If only this were our first thou and desire, then everything else would happen according to his his timing as he sees it to be for bringing wholeness to his child God's ways are not our ways. He can see the present and futur at once. He wants his children to receive the full benefits, lacl

nothing. This world is so "instant" in everything—like an immature baby. We must move beyond our personal wants, time frames, and expectations and enter the relationship with our Father with humility and pureness of heart, waiting to receive what he has for us, to fill us up and give us a touch from the heavenly realms. These earthly bodies are restricted and influenced by worldly things, but our spirit man rules and reigns the physical body, if we are walking in obedience and love with our Creator. Jesus died on the cross so that we have salvation and so that we have his power within us to accomplish everything he has for us to do in this time and place to prepare us for eternity. All will be made right and whole. Consider Philippians 4:12: "I know both to be abased, and I know how to abound: every where and in all things I am instructed both to be full and to be hungry, both to abound and to suffer need." This scripture teaches us that we become our true selves in Christ by being content in every situation. Humility leads to contentment, which allows us to have peace in trials and to be thankful in times of prosperity.

Humility also brings unity, because when we are humble we are not thinking more highly of ourselves but are serving others, knowing that we all have the same value. When we don't think of anyone as less than ourselves but equal in our maker's eyes, it changes how we

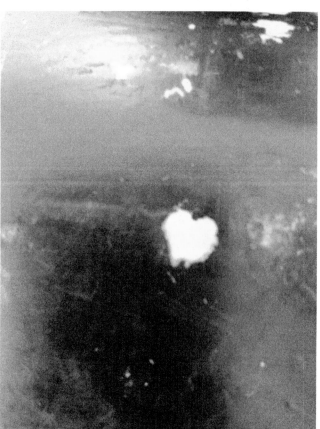

or those around us in everyday life. One afternoon, I was sit-
at our kitchen table and saw something small dried on the table
tried to wipe it off. A piece broke off, leaving remains in the
e of a heart. We have to be made small and be humbled through
service to the one who truly holds all that is infinitely great so
he is seen for who he is, a royal King who holds us all together.

nany dear friends and family have been blessed with heart mo-
ts. One day, I received a text message with a picture from a dear
d who'd encountered God while on vacation. She'd gone for a qui-
alk on the beach where she had prayed about some circumstances
er own life to the Lord, and as she stopped briefly, she looked
n and saw a heart-shaped shell. When thinking about what God
made, I'm reminded of the first line of Genesis 1:31: "And God
every thing that he had made, and, behold, it was very good."

ited the same friend at another time. While we were catching up
/hat had been going on in our lives, she asked me how the book
going, as she always does, and as I looked down to respond, I saw
art shape scratched out on her well-loved kitchen table. Don't
t out things that are not beautiful to some. To be worn shows
True friendship doesn't seek personal gain. I am reminded of
ippians 2 where we should do nothing out of selfish ambition or
conceit, but rather with humility to value others above ourselves.
is one of those beautiful, rare friends who lives her life in this
Instead of putting on airs, she lifts others up in true service.

stepsister Alecia saw an acorn top as she was walking, hav-
prayed earlier for God's strength in some personal areas of her
The occasion reminds me that everyone's triumphs and fail-
are settled in Christ alone. He takes our pieces and makes
n whole. Everything is put together for our good. Colos-
s 1:17 teaches us, "And he is before all things, and by him all
gs consist." I've had so many occasions where God has blessed
family through the heart sightings. After eating strawber-
, my son saw this on his plate. Jesus wanted to bless Hayden
because. God presents himself at every corner to my family.

iesians 4:2 reminds us how to treat one another: "With all low-
ss and meekness, with longsuffering, forbearing one another in
." Being humble and gentle bearing with one another in love, this
pture describes the heart of my son, Hayden, so well, and it reminds
how our hearts should be positioned to walk in likeness of Christ.

not that God is holding his hand of provision or answers all of
time when our prayers aren't answered according to our time-
and thinking. Our long-suffering God wants our patience so
he can reveal to us the inner work he wants to do in our hearts
ough the process of our prayers being answered. It requires that
be in a posture of yielding and obeying to him during the wait.

want to listen for what he wants us to do in the waiting. He has a
iter work and purpose he is threading together. Humility allows us
ay, "I don't know it all, and I need God for everything in my life to be

whole and healthy." It's his plan, not our own. He is enough. If we can let
that settle into our bones, our burden will be lightened. Gratitude will
become our safe haven where we can be thankful for the here and now.
Luke 6:35 teaches us, "But love ye your enemies and do good, and
lend, hoping for nothing again; and your reward shall be great,
and ye shall be the children of the Highest: for he is kind unto the
unthankful and to the evil." These commands are not easy by any
means. It is how my mom taught her children to live. This would
prove to be so painfully difficult to do with my mom's husband during the months I cared for her. With Christ, however, no matter what
evil or ugliness we are faced with, he will give us the grace to do it.

Jesus came and took the fall so that we can know God and be for-
given. This is love. Love gives. Therefore, we give our lives as a living sacrifice. His royal love has no bounds. We shouldn't define
others by our own perceptions and stereotypes. Such boundaries
create division and negativity. Fear, judgements, unforgiveness, selfishness, and pride are the walls that keep us focused on ourselves.
God will use all things to call us to a life of living for others and to
build our trust in him. The enemy is the author of confusion and
division. God is the author and finisher, however, of our faith when
we obey him! We should be willing to learn from other's life experiences and understand where they are in their own life journeys.

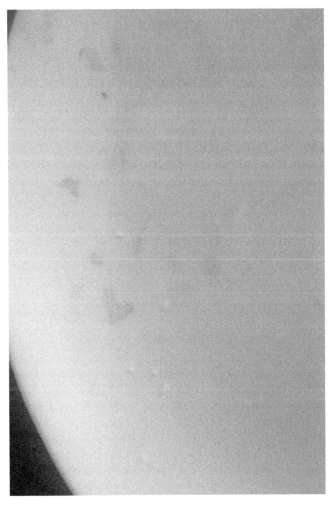

JESUS CAME AND TOOK THE FALL SO THAT WE CAN KNOW GOD AND BE FORGIVEN. THIS IS LOVE.

♥

Our differences are to be embraced and celebrated within the will of God. Even when we disagree, we should look at others the way Christ sees them, showing respect and kindness. For me, the goal is to have a faith that is not in offense. To be in that place where I don't let what others say affect me. I try to see others as they are, where they are, and to not take their words and actions personally. I try to accept them, shortcomings and all.

We will carry what we accept. We are here to encourage each other and support one another in our walk with God. Freedom is what a relationship with Christ is—freedom from things that hold us down and give us heaviness that we can't shake, freedom for forgiveness, and freedom to forgive ourselves and others. Pride wants to hold onto offense, but humility gives forgiveness. We have to keep our focus on humility so that we can keep our attention on our inner workings of our hearts with the Lord. Sometimes that does mean guarding one's heart and drawing boundaries with someone in one's life. God will show you how to guard your heart every step of the way. Everyone has honor in humility, because everyone is being respected and valued, regardless of his or her differences.

God's ways are higher and different from our ways, which means that when Christ's followers are walking out their lives, listening to their Creator, others need to suspend judgment. He knows every detail. Our relationship with God is personal but meant to share so that others will find him. Judgement happens too often in the church, too. It is a trap to suffocate joy, unity, and peace. When Christians are being legalistic and not letting God's love lead, such ways should be a red flag for us to make choices to get into God's presence and to be strengthened where we are weak. A posture of humility needs always to be first. Jesus gave this example when he walked the earth.

God is relational and has a Father's heart toward his children. In or God, author John Bevere describes how the ones who see Go life are the ones who keep his commandments. Bevere remind of the scripture John 14:19 and 21, "Yet a little while, and the v seeth me no more; but ye see me: because I live, ye shall live als . / He that hath my commandments and keepeth them, he it is loveth me: and he that loveth me shall be loved of my Father, a will love him, and will manifest myself to him." A relationship Jesus is the greatest most satisfying relationship you will ever

It is clear we see God at work through the hearts of people and hearts we see in our lives, if we are close and obedient to him and eyes to see. God sent me a present inside a cabbage after I cut it c Is Christ enough as we walk through hard times and good tii

Proverbs 29:23 speaks of pride and humility: "Pride brings a pe low, but the lowly in spirit gain honor." To be lowly in spirit m you are submitting to honoring God and those around you first. Y not boastful about yourself, your opinions, and your accomplishm We have all been around people who are high on themselves, and not enjoyable. I'm sure that we've all been guilty of this at some t

God honors those who give him the honor. He is the one wh due it. He is the good in each of us. Those that love around us because are God's precious gifts. We can learn from them and c into our lives. In the service we do that others do not see is when feel God's love lifting us up and doing things within us that are and irreplaceable. I will never regret laying down my daily life du the months I cared for my mom. Sacrifice for sharing God's lo the only time in my life when I have felt the most alive and comp in my purpose.

CHAPTER 5

———

HEART BEATS

♥ one.

When I am faced with a big decision or I am wrestling with unsure outcomes, I first make a quiet space to be in God's presence and then I commit myself to listening. He will answer us in his own time. For it is in the waiting, that we learn how to follow our God with a humble heart, and we learn how to bring glory to our King.

♥ two.

Contentment is the opposite of our world system. Play some worship music, hang on every word, and concentrate on steering your heart and mind into his presence. Allow him to show you his goodness, which brings you total contentment through all things.

WHAT IS GOD SAYING TO ME TODAY?

CHAPTER 6

STRUGGLES
Repairer of the Breech

My mom learned later in life that ungodly suffering doesn't change people's hearts; only God can do that. What does ungodly suffering mean? It means suffering at one's own will. Mom suffered wounds that were not healed in her heart. We as his children were made to love and to be loved and cherished. We have to protect our own hearts from things that would entrap us and possibly destroy us. Proverbs 22:24–25 tells us how to avoid a trap: "Make no friendship with an angry man; and with a furious man thou shalt not go. / Lest thou learn his ways and get a snare to thy soul." God's word is clear about how to avoid this particular struggle in life, not to bind ourselves with someone who is already entrapped in anger.

Each of our hearts can be healed by being with the one who brings healing. Isaiah 58:12 instructs us on the next generation: "You shall raise up the foundations of many generations, and you shall be called the Repairer of the Breach, the restorer of paths to Dwell In." This scripture explains rebuilding the foundations of generations with the same character, faith, and righteousness with which God builds. As we read in many Bible stories, every time man tried to build without God, man failed. We are made in his likeness to bear fruit of who he is.

We were all playing outside in the driveway one afternoon during the second year of mom's passing, as we do most afternoons, and my daughter ran toward me saying, "Mom, I found a heart." As she guided me to the spot, I was astounded that right in the middle of our driveway, etched out in the concrete, was a heart shape! I thought of 1 Corinthians 2:9: "But as it is written, Eye hath not seen, nor ear heard, neither have entered into the heart of man, the things which God hath prepared for them that love him." These hearts and the timing of their revelations to us and to our family and friends are the deep things of God being revealed to those who love him. There are no limits with God.

My husband and I were having a conversation about how to [...] with a particular issue, and after discussing and coming into ag[...] ment about what we were praying for to resolve the situation, I [...] water on the floor that had formed in a heart shape after he e[...] the shower. I thought of Jeremiah 24:7: "I will give them a hea[...] know Me, for I am the Lord; and they will be My people, and I [...] be their God, for they will return to Me with their whole he[...]

Another wonderful heart sighting happened in a bathroom; [...] time for my stepsister Alecia, who sent me a picture of tooth[...] in the sink, shaped like a heart. The Lord quickly reminded m[...] Jeremiah 29:13: "And ye shall seek me, and find me, when ye [...] search for me with all your heart" Her eyes and heart have [...] opened to seeing God through the hearts. What would God sa[...] you if you asked him to come close and be near to your heart? All [...] have to do is seek and knock, and you will enter into his prese[...]

Sometimes God is orchestrating things for our benefit even w[...] it is out of inconvenience. Such was a time on Mother's Day a[...] took my mother-in-law out to eat. We'd experienced table rese[...] tion troubles. When the hostess finally sat us, my husband looke[...] and said, "Look what's above us!" In the struggle of missing my n[...] on Mother's Day, God met me there. Hebrews 10: 35–36 teache[...] "Cast not away therefore your confidence, which hath great rec[...] pence of reward. / For ye have need of patience, that, after ye [...] done the will of God, ye might receive the promise." When we [...] dure our struggles and trust God's timing, we receive God's prom[...]

My husband and son go on a father-son weekend trip every [...] As I was writing this book, my daughter and I decided to partak[...] some fun activities while they were away. On one outing, we vis[...] a putt-putt center, a new place for us, before going out to din[...]

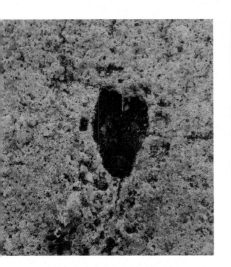
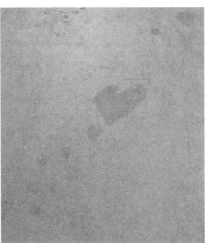
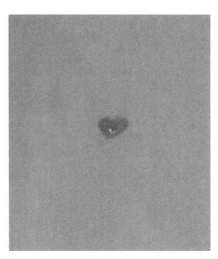

On the way there, I told my daughter that we were going to go eat at Sitty's favorite restaurant. She was excited and said, "I wish Sitty could be here and have fun with us. She would love it!" As we played putt-putt, we came up to a hole where my daughter saw a perfectly heart-shaped leaf on the green. There were no other leaves anywhere to be seen. We just laughed, and I said, "Well, I think Sitty is here. How cool is that?" Then we walked to the next practice hole to find the actual green was in the shape of a heart. We were amazed, and I was so thankful to God for comforting my daughter's heart and revealing himself to her in her process of grieving. Such love is this!

My girlfriend who'd had the heart in the bottom of her coffee cup was baking cookies a year later and opened the carton to find a heart shape on an eggshell. She had recently been through one of the hardest times in her life, building a new business with her husband while processing rejection and pain from people whom she thofught were the most trustworthy. She walked through it with such faith and grace. She faithfully held onto the promises of God in her life. The scripture of 1 John 4:18 tells us to reject fear during the hard times: "There is no fear in love; but perfect love casteth out fear: because fear hath torment. He that feareth is not made perfect in love." God showed my friend his royal love that day.

I think often of 1 John 4: 11–12, which says, "Beloved, if God so loved us, we ought also to love one another. / No man hath seen God at anytime. If we love one another, God dwelleth in us, and his love is perfected in us." God continued to show Alecia his royal love, one day sending her a lovely surprise in her M&M bag, and a heart shape in a butternut squash, ready and waiting for her as she cut it open. Alecia

had one of the hardest, but most rewarding, years of her life. She prayed that God would show her the hearts and did he ever, before the start of her challenging year, during, and continuing forward. She has many photos documenting her encounter with our beyond-incredible, yet most intimate God. My story is your story and everyone's story, similar or different. God wants to reveal himself to us all, and he will, if we will seek him and make space in our hearts to meet with him.

Alecia has felt the sting of isolation and rejection from loved ones and those she should be able to count on the most. She was reunited with her daughter after six years. It was out of great tragedy, but God has held her in his arms every step. He has given her the bravery to help her daughter recover and know the one who made her before her mother's womb. These two people have learned that God brings good out of bad, if we seek him first and trust in his promises. Walking out our faith and being carried through our struggles in life is not always neatly packaged or orderly. It is a sloppy mess at times and has highs and lows. With God's grace and love, though, we can overcome and raise the next generation to higher eternal ground.

GOD WANTS TO REVEAL HIMSELF TO US ALL, AND HE WILL, IF WE WILL SEEK HIM AND MAKE SPACE IN OUR HEARTS TO MEET WITH HIM.

♥

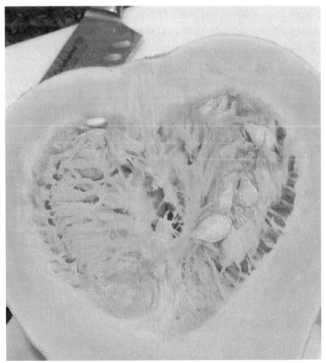

A friend of mine was walking down a sidewalk and saw a heart-shaped rock sitting alone on the path. Though her day was difficult and upsetting, she was met with encouragement. Crossing the same path later, she discovered the rock gone. Our hearts are precious gifts worth guarding from other hurting hearts. It is OK to know when to share our hearts wholly and when to just be an encourager. We are instructed in Proverbs 4:23, "Keep thy heart with all diligence; for out of it are the issues of life."

My mother-in-law, Kathy, had a tree cut down in her backyard, and when they were about to grind the stump, she noticed the shape of the tree. A heart! So, she had a piece of it cut for me. We knew this was God's encouragement for her. The Lord was letting her know that he was with her through difficult times, as she walked by faith. We met when I was fifteen, and she is like my second mom and such a blessing in my life. Zachariah 2:8 shows us God's eyes are fixed on us: "For thus saith the Lord of hosts; After the glory hath he sent me unto the nations which spoiled you: for he that toucheth you toucheth the apple of his eye." We are the apple of the Lord's eye and he loves us with a perfect love that never takes his eye from us.

My mom's friend Christine, who helped me care for Mom, was experiencing a difficult time, so she came to my home and we prayed and talked about the situation. She is an incredible woman of faith and has such a heart for God. After we'd prayed, I noticed I needed to wash off my coffee spoon rest. I picked it up to wash it and noticed the heart-shaped coffee stain. It has never happened again. I use it every day. We were overjoyed, and we thanked God for confirming his goodness and provision in all things. In Romans 12:2 we are reminded not to be confirmed of this world, but to be transformed by the renewing of our minds so that we can prove

what is the good and acceptable will of God. God's word renews mind so that we can change, no matter what harmful things we have learned growing up. We don't have to accept our earthly sh comings. We are made whole and perfected through his living w

My sister-in-law Keira sent a photo to me after noticing her uum cord while vacuuming. This sighting happened a week be she started having complications with her pregnancy. Later, as stood in faith for her baby's health, I reminded her of what had showed her in that moment. I am happy to report that she a healthy baby boy. During the weeks of the unknown with pregnancy, her husband and my brother, Matthew, cut the st er from an apple for her and saw a lovely heart shape remai

OUR HEARTS ARE PRECIOUS GIFTS WORTH GUARDING FROM OTHER HURTING HEARTS. IT IS OK TO KNOW WHEN TO SHARE OUR HEART WHOLLY AND WHEN TO JUS' BE AN ENCOURAGER.

♥

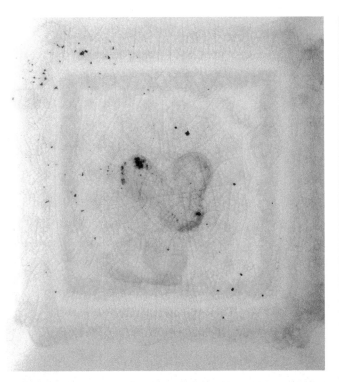

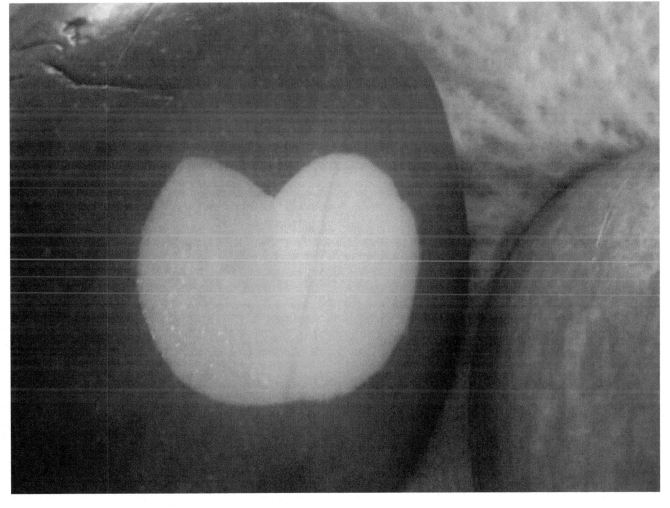

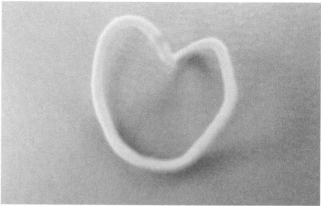

A number of other sightings have come during times of trial. I was on the phone with Alecia sharing with her about the results of a very difficult situation we were going through as a family, and as we talked about Mom, a piece of heart-themed art was in front of her. Later that day, my daughter took her ponytail out and sat her rubber band on the armrest in the car and said, "Mommy, there's a heart." God is with us, and we can feel and see him in our struggles, if we pay attention. While visiting a dear friend at the close of the summer season, I was surprised with a rock she'd found at a park.

She told me how she had looked down to see it among the other rocks in front of her. To her surprise, while we visited we went outside her front door to feel the cool weather and my son looked down to see a heart-shaped leaf on my friend's porch. We looked for the tree that grew leaves in this shape but could not find it. This single leaf was the only one! She got her own heart that day. God was encouraging her and all of us in that moment! He never leaves us nor forsakes us!

Alecia sent me a photo of a heart-shaped mark on her tile floor after noticing it in her house. How might God want to reveal himself to you? Take the time to be quiet and seek him. He will speak to your heart in the way that is perfect for you.

At Christmas, my sister-in-law Cheryl, while cooking a dish to bring for Christmas dinner, discovered her own heart blessing after slicing a potato. He knows our struggles and wants to comfort us at all times. Christmas without Mom is always hard.

Another time, a dear friend, who'd been experiencing some big changes in her life that included uprooting her family to move across the country, came to visit. After visiting old friends and spending time with those she'd missed terribly, she received her heart sighting after opening her sandwich at Chick-fil-A. He is our sustainer in all things! Faith during our struggles leads us: "For we walk by faith, not by sight" (2 Corinthians 5:7). We walk by complete trust in Christ, not by how our circumstances look or how much information we attain.

WE WALK BY COMPLETE TRUST IN CHRIST, NOT BY HOW OUR CIRCUMSTANCES LOOK OR HOW MUCH INFORMATION WE ATTAIN.

♥

"I WILL LOVE THEE, O LORD, MY STRENGTH" PSALM 18:1

♥

I remember when it was the weekend of my birthday, and I was missing Mom and the special way she always celebrated my birthday. On the Friday night of the weekend, my husband and I attended a fundraiser for the American Heart Association. This was our first time attending. I found it amazing that the event happened to be on my birthday weekend and that they gave stones as a gift, each upon which a heart had been painted. The family of a young boy who'd overcome so many obstacles regarding the health of his heart gave this stone to every person who'd helped their child along the way. My mom was definitely a person who helped me so much in life.

My niece saw a heart on the tree in front of her neighbor's yard. This young lady has been through so much at a young age. Now, she is experiencing her Creator for the first time. The scripture John 15:13 comes to mind: "Greater love has no one than this, that he lay down his life for his friends." My niece is learning about the love her Father in heaven has for her and, in turn, she is able to share that love with her friends through the hearts. When we put others before ourselves, we are showing them that they are loved. Jesus loved us so much that he laid down his life so that we can know his perfect love. Our Creator is there for my niece and for us all, wherever we may be in our walk with God. God showed me this truth so profoundly when

I stopped at a restroom while traveling home from a family visi[t] saw a tile with a heart shape broken out of it in a filthy restroom d[ur]ing a pit stop. We had traveled to visit family and spend time wit[h] very special uncle who'd been having some health problems. He is [the] most special uncle a girl could ask for, and he means the world to [me.]

It is hard to see a loved one go through difficulties when you can't h[elp] fix their troubles. When God revealed his unwavering love in the station restroom, I thought, *Lord, right now?* He quickly remind[ed] me, though, that he is with us in the dark, sad, not-so-pleasant pl[ac]es. No place is too dark or too sad for his love. His light can br[eak] through any place, anytime. His love is everywhere. Don't ever co[unt] him unavailable.

He was available to me one day as I picked up a big branch that [had] fallen in the yard. As I walked, I looked down and saw a dead, bro[wn] leaf. I noticed quickly the heart shape broken out in the middle of [the] leaf. I had been in prayer that week for situations that seemed d[ead] and beyond life, but we know that God can return life to anything[, a] broken marriage, a broken heart, any broken relationship, hurt, p[ain,] or loss. He brings the dead back to life! He gives the breath of l[ife]

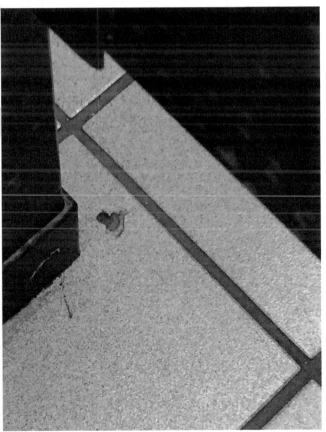

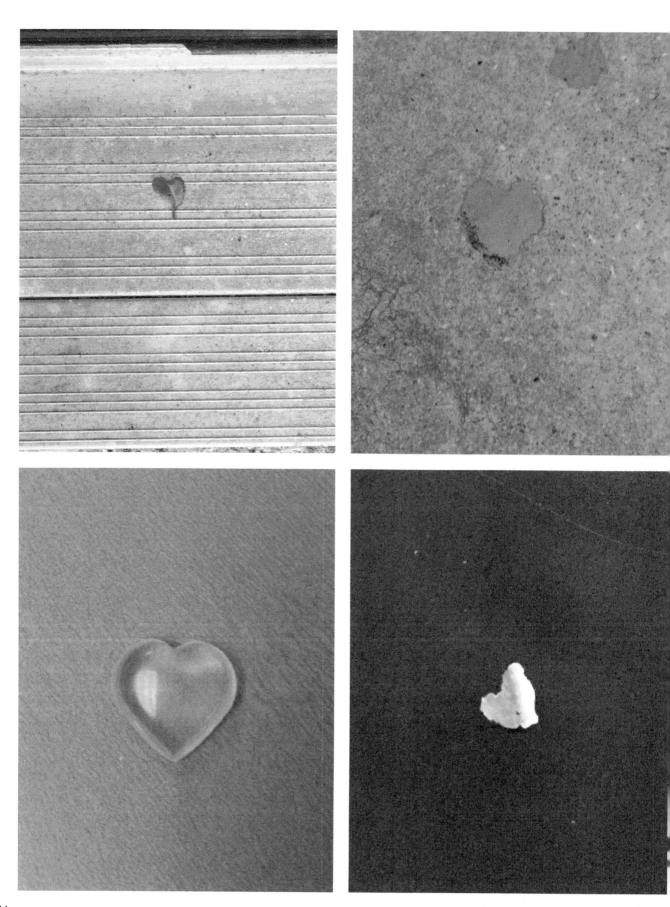

IT IS IN THE WAITING THAT GOD SHOWS UP TO ENCOURAGE US AND KEEP OUR EYES ON HIM AND HIS CAPABILITIES.

♥

spoke to my heart to share this heart sighting with my niece, as had experienced the loss of a parent. This leaf came into my on a difficult day for her, to bring my niece his life on the versary of her father's passing. God knows *all* of our hurts. Oh! he loves.

days before the anniversary of my mom's return to the heavens, art-shaped leaf was on our doorstep. Typically, we don't use this door. On this particular day, however, my husband was fixing doorbell, so we were both on the front door stoop. Repeatedly, ugh the heart revelations, God has reminded me that he is with n times of pain. Always!

day after the anniversary of Mom passing into forever, this t stone and heart stain on the floor of a restaurant were sweet to a friend, who then shared it with me. We all have our own tions that lead us into prayer and reliance on God. He speaks ach of our hearts, if we will listen. He spoke love to her and me in two beautiful moments. The first encounter was in a restaurant, as my friend bent over to pick something up and saw a heart in the concrete floor. The second occasion came on a playground on the same day, when a small child brought my friend a pink, heart-shaped stone. The child had no knowledge of the heart story.

God sees our struggles. I was talking on the phone with a friend when I looked up to see a tiny crumb in the shape of a heart on my coffee table. We were talking about difficult times in our lives but that God is with us. He sees our struggles and knows how each one will work out in his perfect timing, if we trust him. It was a great reminder for us that we are not always supposed to be a part of fixing circumstances in our lives. It is in the waiting that God shows up to encourage us and keep our eyes on him and his capabilities. Holding our peace is just as important, keeping ourselves out of the way so that our struggles do not worsen. He is the ultimate repairer, and he can make all things new.

CHAPTER 6

HEART BEATS

♥ one.

Write in a journal two good things that have come out of your past struggles. These may be blessings that you had not considered previously but, in the end, worked out for your betterment.

♥ two.

Can we ever really appreciate the mountaintops in our life without ever having gone through the valleys? When you are on a mountaintop, reach out to someone around you and do an act of service: take them to lunch, help them with something, or give them a special gift. After all, it's not always just about us.

WHAT IS GOD SAYING TO ME TODAY?

CHAPTER 7

SEEING GOD
In the Unlikely Places

Seeing God really is about opening ourselves to being still and receiving his wisdom and knowledge. His handiwork is all around us, and our God can use anything he wants to reveal himself to his people. We want so badly to put him in a box or label him according to some subgroup or type. He is, however, just too amazing, too miraculous, too astonishing, and too vast for that. When I started to share God's movement in my life, the heart testimony, with my friends and family—in amazement and humbleness at how incredible and loving our God is—I came to a greater understanding of his presence.

A few weeks later, I returned to a special spot at the beach with my mom's friend, where previously I'd shared the heart testimony with her, and another amazing occurrence took place. As we were walking across the street to head onto the beach, she said, "You're missing it!" There was a heart drawn in chalk on the road at our access. I walked right over it, not seeing it until she pointed it out. I wasn't paying attention. How many times in our busy lives do we tune out to things around us? We are bombarded with so much in our culture on a daily basis. Perhaps we just miss God or God moments around us.

Coming home from an outreach at my church one night, I was thinking about Mom and how much I missed hearing her voice and being with her. I thought about her funny comments and beautiful face. Pulling into the driveway, I looked up to see around the moon were dark blue clouds making the shape of a heart. I just wanted to cry out of joy. What a special, sweet, sacred gift to a hurting heart. His love is relentless and perfect.

While in the mountains, we were kayaking with the kids when we looked up in the sky and saw another heart shape in the clouds. We all laughed and someone said, "Yep, we know Sitty is with us, and thank you, God!" It was such an encouragement for our children.

My children were working through their own grieving, and God knows when we need an extra nudge of love.

When we try, we can connect moments of his royal love all around us. One day, the kids were playing outside, and they started to talk about how much they missed Mom. As we walked, I crossed the yard to pick up a stick. My mouth dropped! There was a branch from a pine tree in the shape of a *J*, a cross clearly at the top. I learned years later that pine trees form these crosses at the top of the trees at certain times of the year. I'd never known that, and I'd certainly never had one fall in my yard from our pine trees, but it did in perfect timing. Moreover, it had made a *J* shape. Mom's first name was Janet, and, of course, she is with Jesus! It was such a special moment with my kids and a witness to them of God's presence. The presence of God was with us during the difficult first Christmas without Mom. We were remembering her constantly and all the excitement she had for Christmas. We talked of how she decorated her Christmas tree each year in heart decorations, and how she always shared that Christmas was about Christ's love for all people.

That year we had purchased a new version of a popular Christmas storybook, which we read each year, because the old copy was falling apart. In the new book, toward the end, was a picture of a heart in a box, not an original image in the previous edition. The story shares about knowing Christ—like a butterfly coming out of a dark cocoon into the light and a new life, so we do too. The book goes on to share that our stained hearts are made new and we are immune from death. Once again, we were amazed by the method and the moment God used to speak to the hearts of his children. God brings all things together with his message of love in the most unlikely of places.

HOW MANY TIMES IN OUR BUSY LIVES DO WE TUNE OUT TO THINGS AROUND US? WE ARE BOMBARDED WITH SO MUCH IN OUR CULTURE ON A DAILY BASIS. PERHAPS WE JUST MISS GOD OR GOD MOMENTS AROUND US.

♥

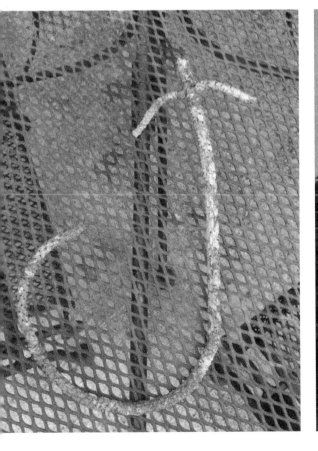

Like a butterfly emerging from a dark, tight cocoon,

You are born to new life, from death now immune.

To be born again means your stained heart is made new.

God's power is yours to know right and what's true.

God also was with us at my son's first piano recital. At home, Hayden had shared with me that he wished Sitty were at the recital to listen to him play the piano. I told him, "You never know; she may be looking down and watching." After the recital, my daughter was playing on the back patio near my husband and me and found three bells topped with heart shapes tucked under the stairs. How unlikely is that? My husband did not know of my previous conversation with our son. I took the bells to Hayden and said, "Guess who was watching?" We were all in amazement of our God and his gentle reminders of his love.

My stepsister Alecia noticed a message from Christ in an unlikely place. I bought her a cross bracelet for her birthday and did not realize until she pointed it out that hearts ran alongside the cross. We thought it a special birthday gift with a hidden message. I hope I will never underestimate again the message of love God has for all people. Nothing can keep us from the love of God. As it is written in Romans 8, death, life, angels, demons, our fears, worries, nothing in all of creation or even the powers of hell will ever be able to separate us from the love of God that is revealed in Christ our Lord.

A friend of mine had prayed to see the hearts—to hear from the Lord in that way—and months and months later, she was drinking her coffee and a little in the bottom of the cup had dried into a perfect heart shape. We are told how to minister to one another in 1 Peter 4:10: "As every man hath received the gift, even so minister the same one to an-

other, as good stewards of the manifold grace of God." This scri shares with us that as each one of us has received a gift, we shoul it to serve one another. It's not about who has what gifts and how some we are because of it. This life's richness and fullness is in sh our gifts with each other, helping one another know God is the who gets the glory and deserves all the honor. Improbable, yes. H ever, that's where God moves at times. We get to see him in his

One day, I was cleaning our bathroom and noticed in the bo shells a heart patch. I remembered my mom having it at some p but somehow it had been placed in the bowl of shells. I knew it v there the last time I'd been in the bathroom, which was in the she stayed while I cared for her. I still don't know how it got t but it was there. What we call unbelievable, God calls believ

God meets us wherever we are. I was thinking about Mom one feeling emotional and sad, wishing she were still here and tel God how much I missed her, when I got a response email, comp with a heart icon at the bottom, from a person who works at children's school. Through this five-year journey, I hope that I sealed forever in my mind how scripture tells us that God's timi always perfect. He has made this obvious time and time again— in the most unlikely places.

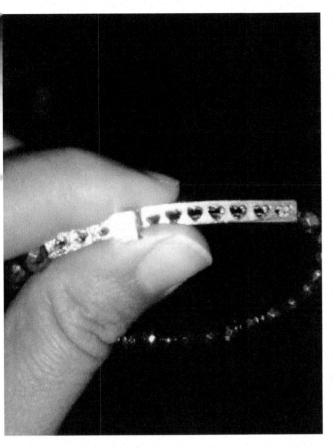

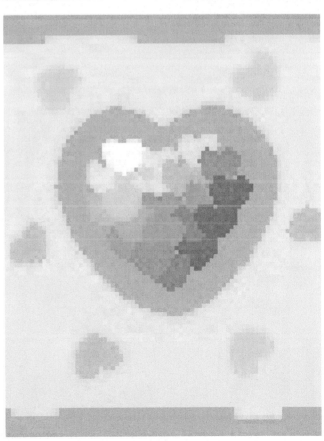

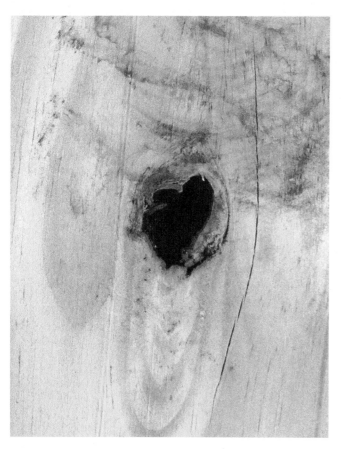
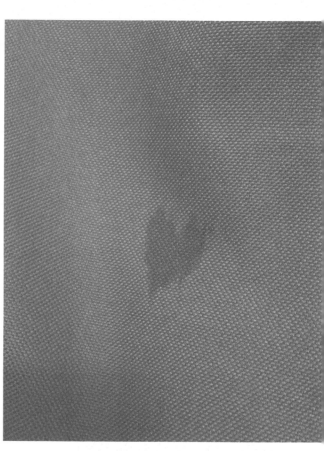

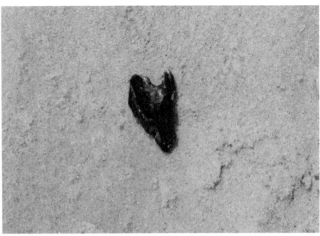
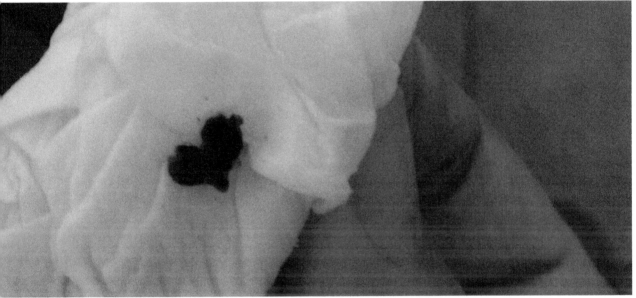

wants to reveal himself to each of us in our own special way. My [husb]and and son worked on a tree fort together. Months later, he saw a [hear]t on one of the pieces of wood. Another time, we were at my son's [base]ball game and Hayden had just taken a drink from his water bottle [and] one drop fell on the chair. My husband came over a few minutes [later] and noticed a dark spot that caught his eye. He looked down to [see i]t was a heart-shaped water drop. I showed it to my son and ex[plai]ned, "God and Sitty are looking down and cheering you on, buddy!" [My] children have been so blessed by the hearts. On my son's birthday, [my] daughter was eating her ice cream and saw a heart shape in her [ice c]ream cup. When we think of unlikely places, we think "unlikely" [beca]use to us it seems insignificant, small, mundane, common, gen[eral,] or casual. Our creator doesn't view anything as such, because the [scal]e of his love is so great and is unlimited; therefore, he uses all to [conv]ey his heartbeat for his kids. Psalms 31:24 reminds us, "Be of [goo]d courage, and he shall straighten your heart, all ye that hope in [the] Lord." Our hope is in him, and we are so thankful for his gifts.

At dinner one evening, the kids noticed a special gem as we began to eat. I have never seen this kind of caddy ever. Yes, Lord, let my children learn to see you in all of life around them. Let them be tender and open to your expressions of love.

God joins us in every step. He was with us on the beach as Alecia, who'd come for a visit, and I walked one afternoon. As we searched for shark's teeth, she found two heart-shaped shells on the beach! Another heart moment involves Alecia, who was cleaning out her microwave and saw a heart shape in the food bits she'd wiped down. I consider this an unlikely, beautiful reminder for us all. Our serving comes in all different ways and is all valuable to Christ. Even in the sometimes mundaneness of serving our families and running our households, God can bring us a message of encouragement in so many different ways, reminding us of how valuable we are to him. God calls us to serve one another just as his son did when he walked the earth. Mark 10:45 compels us to serve: "For even the Son of man came not to be ministered unto, but to minister, and to give his life a ransom for many."

When we open our eyes to see, we look and find Christ. My daughter saw a heart message in a bowl of ice cream. She'd just started to eat the creamy treat and noticed this piece of heart chocolate on the side. What a sweet delight from God!

Sometimes God speaks to us through the same way twice. My dear friend from Virginia had another gift on her front porch. A single, beautiful, heart-shaped leaf. We can miss his voice at times or be uncertain, but he will speak again. He never gives up on us. Job 33:14 declares, "For God speaketh once, yea twice, yet man perceiveth it not." I've noticed that God often comes to us when we are close to nature.

My daughter was on spring break and we went to our favorite beach spot for the afternoon. As we exited the car to walk to the beach, a heart-shaped stain was next to us. Christ's imprint of grace is on her heart forever. Titus 2:11 reminds us, "For the grace of God that bright salvation hath appeared to all men."

My husband saw ironwork in the shape of a heart at a market while on a mission trip to Haiti. He has such a love for the people of Haiti, and he wanted to bring me back something that was special to me, a heart. He sent me a photo of the heart on what would have been Mom's birthday. I so admire the beautiful welding by a Haitian artist of the three wise men, star of David, Mary,

Joseph, and baby Jesus with a donkey—all within a heart. A days later, a good friend sent another heart photo to me w eating brunch at a local restaurant. Her heart is after the Fat heart. Faithfully, he has spoken to her. I am humbled by how has shown himself to my friends and family through the he

My sister-in-law, Keira, sent me the most remarkable p to of a heart fungi after attending a school science walk with son. God had a message for the six-year-old and his mo His handiwork of creation. Matthew 22:37–39 reminds us of Lord's commands: "Jesus said unto him, Thou shalt love the I thy God with all thy heart, and with all thy soul, and with all mind. / This is the first and great commandment. / And second is like unto it, Thou shalt love thy neighbour as thy

The beautiful thing about God and having faith in him is that w we experience things that are not likely to happen through our tionship with him, we are strengthened by witnessing his nature faithfulness. God is with us and revels in loving on his children adding joy to their days on this earth. If we have open hearts and to stop and see God in the unlikely places, we will walk humbly happily with our God.

CHAPTER 7

——

HEART BEATS

♥ one.

A good question we can ask ourselves each day is, how can we connect to God today? Through our connecting, we have the ability to see him and his workings, perhaps through a five-minute devotional in the morning or a walk on the beach contemplating our gratitude.

♥ two.

God wants to delight us through our childlike faith and his creation. Ask God to speak to you and show you his unique love notes for you.

WHAT IS GOD SAYING TO ME TODAY?

CHAPTER 8

———

TRUSTING IN HIS PROCESS AND PACE
Hope Revived

As we move through life's different seasons, often we may ask, *Where is God?* and *Why is this happening?* Instead of questioning the timing, I propose we seek him and have eyes to see him in those seasons. We can lay everything at his feet and trust him, knowing that he is the God of hope. He will reveal to you his presence and healing touch, working all things for your good and his glory. *Our savior wants to be our everything first.*

The day before our first Mother's Day without Mom, we were organizing items in our attic and found a book Mom had given us. Inside were two notes she'd written years prior, one to my husband, Erik, and one to me.

Corrine: 12-28-99: Grow in Love—rediscover Love and its fullness. As you do, it will fill you—illness, fear, anxiety, the need to always be on top of things will disappear. Faith will take root and you will blossom into truly a woman of Beauty—lastingly!

Erik: 12-28-99: Your ability to lead has been with you since birth. God gave this to you. He does desire you to use this to its fullest to bless your house and others. However, he is waiting for you to bless his house and knows of your desire to do so. He's waiting—come.

God had spoken these words to her during her quiet time with him, and she had shared it with us in a note. Mom was a beacon of hope in our lives, always reminding us of what God provides and gives freely.

We are not to fear. His perfect love does not involve torment, as 1 John 4:18 states, "There is no fear in love; but perfect love casteth out fear, because fear hath torment. He that feareth is not made perfect in love." God gave us the ability to know right from wrong; however, he doesn't beat his people over the head with fear. Fear is not used

against us, but he is clear on the consequences of our choice shows his people love and grace and that reverential fear is our science and guide to what God has for us and what the count offerings are in this world: fame, selfishness, ego, and material

One of his true offerings is that he offers hope when we trust in I saw this play out in his timing when my son's football seaso starting and we were heading to his first game. My son said, "I I really wish Sitty was here to watch my game. She always ca watch me play sports."

I said, "Well, you never know. Maybe God will let Sitty see game."

As we were pulling into the football field parking lot, I looke and saw a huge heart shape in the clouds.I was floored! Re ber that I said his timing is always perfect?We laughed and praises to the Lord for such compassion and love toward m

My sister-in-law, Keira, has marveled at God's message of hope i heart testimony, as well. One day, she texted me a picture of a r made piecrust she had just placed on top of a pie; in one area heart-shaped cutout. We have all missed Mom so much, and has revealed himself to each of us in his own special way and ti

One time he revealed that we are always in his care was whe children were playing outside and saw, for the first time, a red hea our garage floor, made of some substance spilt on the floor by th vious owners. We had walked right over it countless times since ing into the house. Daniel 4:2–3 ensures us that God will contin move through the generations: "I thought it good to shew the and wonders that the high God hath wrought toward me. / How

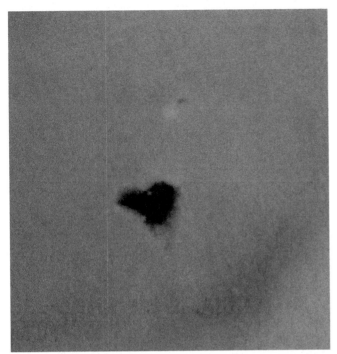
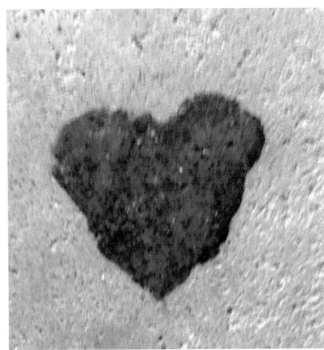
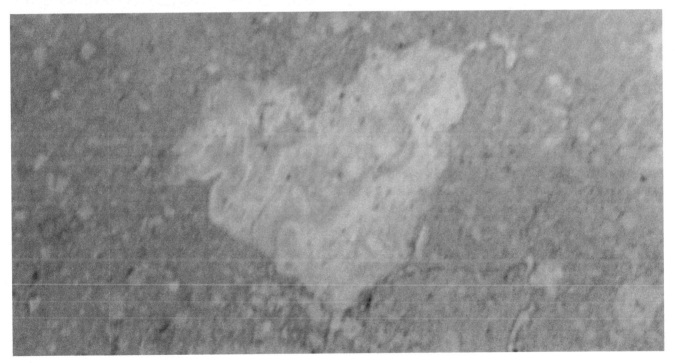

are his signs! and how mighty are his wonders! his kingdom is an everlasting kingdom, and his dominion is from generation to generation." A few years after mom went into eternity, we were in our kitchen one night when my children came running in, shouting, "We see a heart, Mom!" They led me to a spot on our kitchen floor where they'd discovered a perfect heart in the design of the tile. How many times in our lives do we get impatient in the waiting? We live in a global society that, in effect, says, "I want it today." Through technology, we have unlimited resources at our fingertips, but when it comes to our core and our spirits, God says situations take time and trust. He wants his children to perform the inner work. He wants us to grow in righteousness and faith, and he wants us to show everyone around us what a loving, present Father he is. Before he ever answers a wish list of prayers, he wants to know us and for us to know him. He wants to heal our wounds and hearts from being born into a broken world. He wants us to experience him in our lives. He wants to give us hope and a future—not only in this time and space but forever.

Sometimes, I think, when he really wants us to hear him, he sends messages back-to-back. My stepsister Alecia was making cookies, and a cookie came out in a perfect heart shape. A few days later, while walking into an office, her son noticed a rock on the sidewalk, apparently moved from the nearby rock bed. Her son picked it up and said, "Look, a heart rock, Mommy." Our Creator will speak to little children just as he does to an adult. He is with us all the time and wants to speak through the unlikely. It is part of his process and his pace.

Months later, my brother, Cheth was going on his first mission trip to Haiti, so the family decided to go down to the beach to spend time with him and pray for his trip. As we walked down the beach that night, we found hearts drawn in the sand at least four times. Before spotting the hearts, my brother had been discussing how he wished Mom were here to be a part of the mission work and how he would have loved to talk with her about his trip.

During his mission trip, he met a man in Haiti who handmade hearts from rocks. We had no doubt that Mom was with Cheth on his first mission trip. How God filled my brother with hope reminds me of Ezekiel 36:26: "I will give you a new heart and put a new spirit within you; I will remove your heart of stone and give you a heart of flesh." Mom was with Cheth in spirit on his mission trip, and God's royal love was with us on Grandparents' Day at my children's school. Loren and Hayden had shared all morning that they wished Sitty were with them that day and that they were missing her terribly. After events at their school, we all went to lunch: Erik's parents, our children, and me and Erik. Erik's parents were already sitting in a booth when we arrived. As I was seated, I looked up and realized the only heart artwork in the restaurant was above our table. We knew at this moment that God was with us and that he and Mom were enjoying showing their love.

"I WILL GIVE YOU
A NEW HEART AND PUT
A NEW SPIRIT WITHIN
YOU; I WILL REMOVE
YOUR HEART OF STONE
AND GIVE YOU A HEART
OF FLESH."
EZEKIEL 36:26

♥

On another occasion, for my daughter's birthday, we went to breakfast at her great uncle's restaurant before school. Walking out of the restaurant my daughter said, "Look, Mom, a heart!" Leaves were blowing everywhere and she saw three grouped together, forming a heart shape. She was so thrilled, and she thanked God that he and Sitty were with her on her birthday! He gives us hope and a future.

Later that day, we attended her school play, where she held out her hand and said, "Look what was on the playground today, Mommy. I saved it so I could show you when I saw you!" Her playground is covered in thousands of leaves and she saw this one! "And thou shalt love the Lord thy God with all thy heart, and with all thy soul, and with all thy mind, and with all thy strength: this is the first commandment" (Mark 12:30).

My daughter loves the Lord with all her heart, and so does Alecia. God sent her many heart sightings of hope and encouragement. Over the summer, Alecia went out to a restaurant for her

wedding anniversary and discovered a heart shape on her dinner. Her sighting makes me think of Romans 8:24: "For we are saved by hope: but hope that is seen is not hope: for what a man seeth, why doth he yet hope for?" This verse reminds me that patience and trust is vital. Hope leads to building our patience and reliance on him. He will send us encouragement along the way.

My girlfriend's children heard the heart story at school from Loren, who'd shared about the heart found on her birthday. It made such an impression on their little hearts; weeks later, they were in their backyard and decided they wanted to find heart leaves and started looking. They found quite a few. They have hundreds of thousands of leaves in their backyard, as well. Matthew 18:3 reminds us, "And verily, I say unto you, Except ye be converted, and become as little children, ye shall not enter into the kingdom of heaven." The Lord wants us to come to him with faith like that of a child.

Faith is so important. I couldn't have walked through Mom's illness with her without faith. I remember a time when I was feeling down and God's royal love picked me right back up. I'd gone to pick up take-out dinner one night, and I pulled the napkins out of the bag and found a tiny heart on the napkin. I saw it and thought, *No, that's not a heart.* It was so small. As I looked closer, though, I couldn't believe what I was seeing. The scripture Matthew 17:20 comes to mind: "And Jesus said unto them, Because of your unbelief: for verily I say unto you, If ye have faith as a grain of mustard seed, ye shall say unto this mountain, Remove hence to yonder place; and it shall remove; and nothing shall be impossible unto you." In this scripture, Jesus isn't condemning the disciples' faith. He was trying to show them the importance of faith for the future; instead of looking at the mountain-like obstacles in your life, look to Christ and trust him. Only then will you be able to overcome what stands in your way.

My family and I were driving home from the beach, talking about Mom, and we stopped at a red light. The car in front of us had four hearts on its back windshield. Romans 12:12 gives us instruction on different seasons of our lives: "Rejoicing in hope; patient in tribulation; continuing instant in prayer." The hearts have done just that, given us hope and kept our eyes on Christ, instead of on our pain and the voice of the enemy.

Months later, I was putting some beads my daughter had received from school in her vanity drawer and spied a heart. My sister-in-law, Keira, had given the vanity to my daughter a few months prior because she rarely used it. The amazing part is my mom had refinished the vanity with Keira and given it to her. More amazing still is that I saw the heart on what would have been my mother's birthday! Romans 15:13 fills us with encouragement: "Now the God of hope fill you with all joy and peace in believing, that ye may abound in hope, through the power of the Holy Ghost."

Mom's dear friend Christine, who'd helped me care for Mom when she was sick, gave my children a movie called *The Lost Medallion.* As we watched the movie, one of the actor's lines stood out in reference to our hearts. The line was about trusting one's heart to the one who created it, that our heart is our medallion. A medallion is a beautiful ornamental piece of jewelry. If we treated our heart as medallions, how might we go about in keeping it safe and healthy and in trusting our hearts first to the one who created it? God knows every detail of our hearts, and he knows what is needed for it to work at its best.

While writing these chapters, I have been participating in a Beth Moore study with a good friend. Beth Moore founded the Living Proof Ministries. This particular study was of the book of Daniel. I found it so interesting that Moore's study book teaches on the last days of our times and the heart of the people during these times. She points out a scripture in the study that is such a reflection of our world today: "And because iniquity shall abound, the love of many shall wax cold" (Matthew 24:12). There is God, who wants to make our hearts whole, and then there is the enemy, who wants to fragment and break our heart into pieces, leaving us broken.

In the study, Moore wrote for the reader to think about the importance of prayer, not just for earthly riches but what matters most. She suggests the things that matter most is purpose, satisfaction, godly influence, restoration in our relationships, and for our lives to produce fruit. All of these things depend on prayer. Prayer is what releases things into our lives. When we pray, we are building relationship with God. God calls us his beloved. In Ephesians 1:6, it says that because of grace we are made acceptable in the beloved. God loves each one of us.

Ephesians 5:25 directs us, "Husbands, love your wives, just as Christ loved the church and gave himself for it." The word beloved is defined as a "much-loved person" and "dearly loved"; synonyms include *treasured, prized, adored,* and *cherished.* This is how Jesus loves us. How beautiful. Let that sink in; think about how our actions and words we use toward our loved ones either adores them or tears them down. This is a great reminder for us all to trust in Jesus's pace and process in molding our hearts. In this verse, he commands husbands to love with this deep, authentic, royal love. In Christ's love we are his beloved; therefore, we should express the same with our spouses. We are only able to do that as we walk in relationship with Christ.

I was on the phone talking with Christine, as she shared with me about a difficult situation she was walking through and about how God had met her with encouragement through a stranger, when a car pulled up in front of me at a red light. I couldn't help but notice the bottom of the back window of the truck. When I told her what I was seeing in that moment, we realized that God had given her even more encouragement.

A few weeks later, while at a church event, I met a newcomer. We discussed volunteering and how long I had been at the church. When I explained that I was writing a book and what it was about, the person was so moved by the story that she proclaimed she would see a heart before she left that evening. I said, "Well, if it's God's will, then you will. You know, it's just about having eyes to see him and know how much we are loved."

"NOW THE GOD OF HOPE FILL YOU WITH ALL JOY AND PEACE IN BELIEVING, THAT YE MAY ABOUND IN HOPE, THROUGH THE POWER OF THE HOLY GHOST."

♥

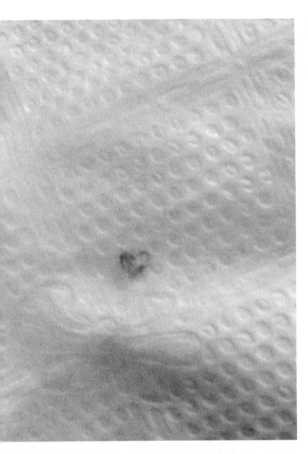

"AND JESUS SAID UNTO THEM, BECAUSE OF YOUR UNBELIEF: FOR VERILY I SAY UNTO YOU, IF YE HAVE FAITH AS A GRAIN OF MUSTARD SEED, YE SHALL SAY UNTO THIS MOUNTAIN, REMOVE HENCE TO YONDER PLACE; AND IT SHALL REMOVE; AND NOTHING SHALL BE IMPOSSIBLE UNTO YOU."
MATTHEW 17:20

The speaker continued, and about twenty minutes later, the person reported that she'd seen a woman wearing heart earrings. She kept trying to show me, but I could not see them. When the speaker finished, I asked, "Which woman has them on?" She showed me, and I remarked, "Hey, I know her." Instantly, it became a special bonding moment between us. If we seek God with pure hearts, he will reveal himself to us. I approached my friend who'd worn the earrings at the end of the night and told her the story. She was just as shocked as I was, and she shared that God had his own message of encouragement that night for her, too. He is always with us.

I quickly thought of a saying I'd heard from Bono: Religion is what you're left with when the Spirit leaves the building. The Holy Spirit in that moment was weaving his message for each of us. How often do we attend church gatherings and not speak or respond to the Holy Spirit knocking on our hearts to share something with others? When we make our encounters with other people more superficial, we miss what the Holy Spirit wants to impart in any given moment. We need to trust his purpose and pace.

Later in the week, I was cleaning up the kitchen, and in passing, I saw a small speck of something that had dried in the shape of a heart. It was so tiny but so profound. That, I thought, is how it is when our hearts are open to God's heart. His presence ushers into where we are, filling the space with his love and light.

Our family went on a road trip for spring break in March. Of course, we always stock the car with a bag of snacks for the road. While driving, I pulled the beef jerky out of the bag to see a heart looking back at me, so tiny and strategically placed on the white freshness pack. I couldn't help but to laugh and thank God for caring so much to remind me of his presence and love. Wrap the thought around your mind that hope does not disappoint, as we are told in Romans 5:5: "And hope maketh not ashamed; because the love of God is shed abroad in our hearts by the Holy Ghost which is given unto us."

We can have great hope as we are filled with the Holy Spirit by taking time to be with Jesus. Your heart can weaken when we have hope deferred, causing us not to feel well and not at peace. Having hope in Jesus, however, and knowing him in relationship, gives our hearts assurance and lasting peace for whatever happens in our daily lives.

CHAPTER 8

—————

HEART BEATS

♥ one.

Rediscover Jesus and the fullness of his love and you will grow in love. Talk with a trusted friend who knows God, or find a local church where you feel at home.

♥ two.

Hope found is freedom discovered. True love is rooted in freedom. How can we choose love today to extend freedom, such as undeserved forgiveness? Then we will be given an anchored hope.

WHAT IS GOD SAYING TO ME TODAY?

CHAPTER 9

─────

FOUND IN
Being a Friend of God

By definition, friendship means a "mutual bond," not a one-sided affection, but a mutual one. A friend is a confidant, a person whom one knows. Do we know Jesus? Do we take time to listen to that still, small voice within us, his spirit. Do we seek him in his word and learn his ways? Do we worship him in giving, song, and serving? Do we ask him first before making a decision? Do we say thank you and acknowledge when we see his provision and protection in our lives? A friend is a two-way street, not one.

To know someone is to partake in walking with them, taking the time to care and extend our hearts. These are all questions I have asked myself at some point in my life. I have fallen short at times, but all we have to do is be purposeful and reconnect to our source of joy and peace. We know only Christ is perfect, but we can be in constant motion toward wholeness, which doesn't end until we are in eternity, when we are in relationship with our Creator.

God speaks to us through our friendships. On my birthday, one of my friends gave me a beaded bracelet. Weeks later, I realized there was a heart on one of the beads.

As our all-knowing friend, God gives us the extra encouragement we need. On my sister-in-law's birthday, she went out for sushi. When the sushi platter arrived, pieces had been formed into a big heart. Restaurant staff did not know it was her birthday.

A week later, my stepsister Alecia was cleaning up her daughter's lunch and a lovely heart-shaped strawberry was on her plate. This is friendship, knowing when our friend needs to hear from us and reaching out in love. Jesus is our friend and knows what's happening in our hearts, before we ever say a word. He met her with this love note as a friend. We need to have obedience because it shows our devotion. Devotion to our all-powerful, all-knowing, loving Creator.

While visiting an out-of-town friend to celebrate his friend's g[...] ation from the police academy, my brother, the friend, and his f[...] went for a walk on the beach. Someone's little girl in the grou[...] toward the dunes and then turned and called for my brother to [...] and see what she had found. It was a heart made out of sea[...] This family had no knowledge of the heart testimony. God ca[...] whatever means necessary to reach the people he loves.

On another occasion, unaware of the heart testimony, a friend [...] brother's sent him a picture of a chip in the shape of a heart. Go[...] use our friendships or complete strangers to meet his children's [...] and show them his love.

AS OUR ALL-KNOWING FRIEND, GOD GIVES US THE EXTRA ENCOURAGEMENT WE NEED.

♥

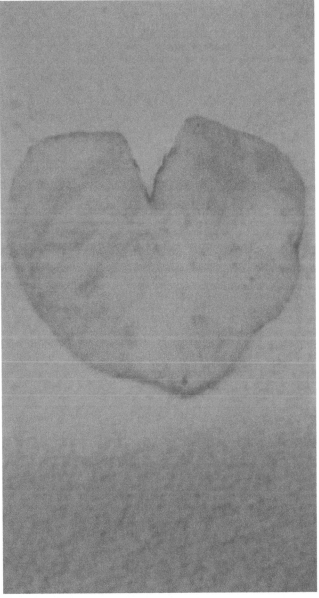

Alecia sent a photo of a heart marking to me after seeing it on her driveway. I think of Proverbs 18:24: "A man that hath friends must shew himself friendly: and there is a friend that sticketh closer than a brother." Alecia shared how she sometimes feels a lack of faith and that she questions herself and if she hears from God. I think we can all say that at some point in our lives. We are all on our own walk with God. I reminded her that I think after she shared her concerns that God was showing himself to her even more through the hearts. I suggested that she might look back on her pictures and remember all the times he spoke to her during her grieving of losing Mom and a close aunt in the same year. During that period, she had also reunited with her daughter, and she and her family were going through that healing process together. It is a journey with God until we die, not a destination.

On the second year of Mom's passing, the family was teasing with each other about who was going to get a heart on their birthday. We were just joking around; yet, it became a comforting thing for us to see the hearts during these times, because, of course, every special occasion in our lives someone was missing. We were all missing Mom. I would laugh one minute, thinking of fun memories, and cry in another, because I just wanted to hug her neck. My children would frequently talk about Mom and ask questions about what she might be doing in heaven and if she thought about them. We had many discussions about heaven and our relationship with Jesus.

On my daughter's birthday that year, as we were walking into school, I glanced up at a friend who was walking in the door as she said happy birthday to Loren and looked at the donuts in my hand. After a second glance, I noticed that she was wearing a hat I had never seen her wear. On the font of the hat was a pink heart. Tears flowed as Jesus was meeting me in that moment. Our friend Jesus knew how much Loren and I missed Mom.

That weekend was my daughter's birthday party. The same friend had bought her a nightgown with a huge red heart on the front awhile before the party. Loren was so happy and so comforted by these beautiful hearts. Of course, after these occasions, I shared the heart testimony with her. The scripture 1 Chronicles 29:18 came to mind: "O Lord God of Abraham, Isaac, and Israel, our fathers, keep this for ever in the imagination of the thoughts of the heart of thy people, and prepare their heart unto thee."

A tennis partner who had never heard the story about the hearts placed a card with a heart on it on my front door step the day before my birthday. I knew God's hand was in this moment. He can do more than we can ever imagine in showing what a friend he is.

Alecia's friend was at a park and saw a heart-shaped cloud in the sky. She sent the photo to Alecia after learning of the heart story. Proverbs 13:20 gets straight to the point on friendship and says to walk with the wise and become wise, for friendship with fools suffers harm. We need to have wisdom when choosing our friendships. The mother of this same friend had passed with cancer a month after my mom. She saw this heart tree stump in the backyard of her new house. Jesus laid down his life for every man. John 15:13 proclaims, "Greater love hath no man than this, that a man lay down his life for his friends." There is no greater love, and Jesus shows us this example by what he did for all of humanity.

A MAN THAT HATH
FRIENDS MUST
SHEW HIMSELF
FRIENDLY: AND
THERE IS A FRIEND
THAT STICKETH
CLOSER THAN A
BROTHER. ”

♥

GOD WILL MOVE ALL THINGS TO YOUR BENEFIT AND GIVE YOU ENCOURAGEMENT WHEN YOU NEED IT.

♥

There is strength in having friends with whom you can pray, encouraging one another without judgement, no matter what they are going through. My girlfriend's mom, who had seen the dried, heart-shaped coffee in the bottom of her coffee cup, had this heart-shaped bit on a mayonnaise-covered spoon while making a dish. She is the friend that walked by faith when having her world completely turned upside down. Proverbs 27:17 tells us, "Iron sharpeneth iron; so a man sharpeneth the countenance of his friend." We sharpen one another in friendships, and we can see some things so much clearer through a trusted friend—and experience these God moments that build our faith.

My niece shared the story of God's love with a friend of hers at school, and the next morning, they saw a heart image on the sidewalk at the bus stop. John 15:14 teaches us, "Ye are my friends, if ye do whatsoever I command you." In my niece's obedience in sharing this move of God through the hearts with her friend, God met them there at another time for them to experience his presence. If we are truly friends with Jesus, then we will do what he asks of us regardless of our apprehensions.

The day before the four-year anniversary of my mom's going home to eternity, a heart-shaped leaf was at my feet as I readied myself to play in a tennis match. In the car on the way to the courts, I'd felt heavy-hearted. I always pray for God to tell Mom how much I love her and miss her. I was doing this even more that day. This was the first time I'd played with this particular team and my first-ever Saturday match. God will move all things to your benefit and give you encouragement when you need it. God calls us friends. "Henceforth I call you not servants; for the servant knoweth not what his lord doeth: but I have called you friends; for all things that I have heard of my Father I have made known unto you" (John 15:15).

Walking in the woods while visiting family after her relative had passed away, my sister-in-law walked upon a beautiful heart shape in a tree. Hebrews 11:1 reminds us, "Now faith is the substance of things hoped for, the evidence of things not seen."

The sister of a good friend of mine sent a photo of heart-shaped sunlight bursting through clouds to her. She was driving down the road and saw this image in the sky. John 16:33 tells us to take heart, he is come: "Howbeit when he, the Spirit of truth, is come, he will guide you into all truth: for he shall not speak of himself; but whatsoever he shall hear, that shall he speak: and he will shew you things to come."

Alecia took a photo of heart-shaped clouds while driving during the week of what would have been my mom's birthday. He is our comfort in time of need. "When I would comfort myself against sorrow, my heart is faint in me" (Jeremiah 8:18).

My family and I pulled out old family videos so that we could see Mom and hear her voice. We all miss her laugh and kind words so much. I don't ever want to forget what her voice sounds like. It may sound odd to want to hear her voice, but hearing it comforts me; it's a voice I have loved since being on this earth. It brings me to tears while writing about it now. The love of a mother is so precious and is such a powerful gift to humanity. It is a bond I don't take lightly, and I am thankful to have the honor of raising two of my very own children. The morning after watching the videos, we made pancakes. One had a special gift in the form of a heart. He knows what we need and when we need it, giving us such love and friendship, just because.

His creation shows his glory! My friend saw a video where a seal swam up to someone's boat, scampering inside. Once again, Jesus was speaking through a friendship of mine. Community with each other is at the core of Jesus's message of love and loving others as yourself. The seal was very curious, and the people let him move all about. Then the seal went right up to the gentleman sitting in the boat and began rubbing the man's side, as a dog would. As the father in the video tells everyone to stay back, he calls someone Corrina. That really pushed it over the edge for me. Not only was the animal's nose in the shape of a heart and that my friend (of all people) saw it on YouTube, but also a girl on the boat was named Corrina? I mean really! You can call it want you want. This, however, I know: our Father hears our prayers and acknowledges us all the time, if we will listen and see. He confirms his love he puts in our hearts. We need his love, and our life depends on his friendship.

My daughter, Loren, had friends over to play. They were all sitting at the kitchen table when she looked up to see that the way she had laid down her jacket had made a heart. What a beautiful moment for her friends to share with her. Loren shared the story of the hearts with her friends, and they were all moved. Their faces revealed their joy, thinking about a connection like this with our God.

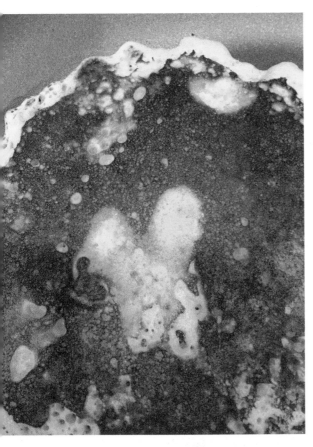

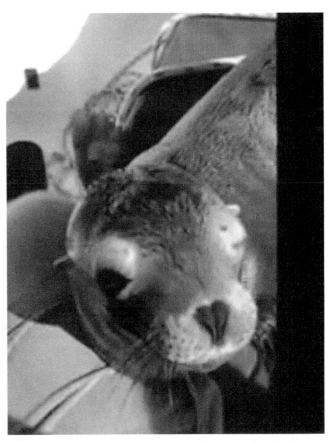

"BLESSED ARE THE PURE IN HEART: FOR THEY SHALL SEE GOD.' MATTHEW 5:8

♥

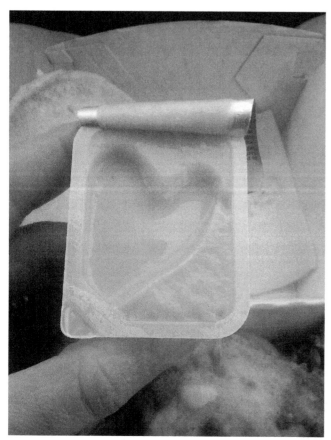
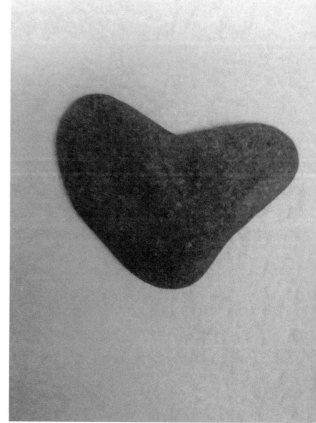

My dear friend had been walking in faith, trusting God for a mighty move in her and her family's life for his fullness and purpose. After answering her and her husband's prayers, he gave her a sweet confirmation of his plans. She found a heart inside her sauce container. Who doesn't love Chick-fil-A? God quickly reminded me of his word. The scripture was Matthew 5:8: "Blessed are the pure in heart: for they shall see God."

God meets us wherever we are. My sister-in-law Cheryl went on an once-in-a-lifetime trip to Tahiti. She had difficult challenges in the last few years, but God has met her and loved her like no one else. After praying for God to show her hearts while she was in Tahiti, she found a beautiful, heart-shaped rock during her trip. She thought she'd lost the rock after putting it in her bag, which upset her tre-

mendously because of what finding it had meant to her and because of the heart story itself.

As she mulled over where it could be and how she could have misplaced it, her boat ride passed by an island. She asked the waiter on the boat the name of the island. He said it's the only island of its kind, because not only is it in the shape of a heart but also it has a lagoon within it that is in the shape of a heart. She was stunned. I felt that it was God making a point. In this life, don't get hung up on what you've lost, no matter how amazing, because you never know what even more amazing thing will replace it. God alone is our Rock and Salvation. When we know Jesus—as represented by this picture—we are never alone. His love is always with us, even when we think we are all alone on an island.

CHAPTER 9

———

HEART BEATS

♥ one.

Jesus is the most reliable friend we will ever have. Pause and think about a friend who would never fail you for a moment. We can include Jesus, by prayer, in our daily decisions, trusting all of who we are to him.

♥ two.

Meditate for a moment on the King of Glory coming to earth as a man and giving his life for people who didn't know him. It becomes a friendship filled with unmerited devotion and endless grace. Think of ways you can extend grace to a friend, and put into action those graces today.

WHAT IS GOD SAYING TO ME TODAY?

CHAPTER 10

MAKE MY HEART CLEAN
Renew a Loyal Spirit

The clean heart is set apart so that it can recognize God. I can't help but to think that in order to see God, we have to have a pure heart. If our hearts are contaminated or mixed with other things that are not of Christ, how can we see clear through to all he wants to show us? Our hearts must be pure and anchored in his ways for us to have eyes to see. The daily conversations I would have with my mom would be about our hearts and how to draw them nearer to this loving, all-knowing God. Mom was determined to teach her children about the Lord, what he thinks and says about us, no matter our own imperfections.

She wanted us to be loyal to him above anything or anyone else. She knew the gifts he had given her in her life and wanted us to know this loving kindness. I enjoyed our long talks about love, honesty, bravery, and God's word, and I miss them dearly. I am determined to pass down the same God-given passion and wisdom to my daughter and son—a bond not easily broken and providing a peace and confidence built on a strong foundation.

God is affirming himself to my children through the wonder of the hearts. Such as when my daughter climbed under our kitchen table and said, "Mommy, there is a heart!"

I said, "Are you sure?"

She went straight to the spot and showed me the perfect image of a heart. Amazing!

Our relationship with our earthly parents, whether great or not so splendid, is a type and shadow of the relationship with our Creator. Except with him, you can have the kind of intimacy your spirit man longs for in every area of your heart. You can attain peace, comfort,

joy, strength, love, hope, and connection that no man on eart provide. God created us in his image; therefore, we bear his qua Genesis 1:27 instructs us, "So God created man in his own i in the image of God created he him; male and female creat them." He made it all for good, but sin in the world has dar and twisted our desires. When we truly seek truth and know h a relationship, our desires align with his. We can't control it. so faithful and good, even in the hard times, that we want to him and give our best to show our appreciation and love for s mighty God.

I was watching a movie and the actor said the heart is har change but the mind can be persuaded. This made me think. I b however, that through reading and hearing the word, we can and renew our minds from the enticements and persuasions c world, the enticements that would pull our hearts away from C Even when we trip up and miss it in life. He has unending grac says, "I love you still. Now, get back up and do this how you kn should be done." Truly, the enemy is the one that comes to div every way possible. If he can use insecurities, judgement, bitte disappointment, and control that people use to mask their hurts he will, to get the eyes of God's people from his consuming lov grace that he extends to everyone everywhere. God extends hi no matter how low you have fallen or how often you have tu away from his truth and wisdom for guidance in your life.

When Jesus returned to heaven, he instructed the disciples tha would have the Holy Spirit, and that the Holy Spirit would emp them to be able to be a witness for him. John 14:26 assures us t is the Holy Spirit who teaches us and gives us the strength to f God's ways. The Holy Spirit is the third person of the Holy Tr God, Jesus, and the Holy Spirit are one. The Holy Spirit dwells i

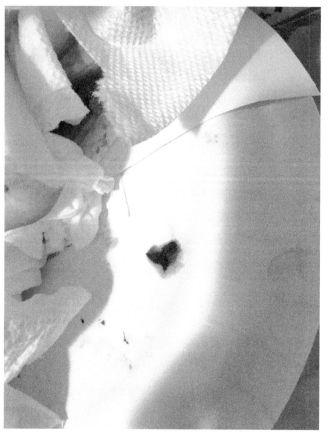

all who receive Jesus into their heart as their Savior. Romans 5:5 ... us that the Holy Spirit pours God's love into our hearts and ... ves us life eternally. Romans 8:10–11 encourages us to know that ... e Holy Spirit is the power God gives believers to overcome their ... orldly circumstances and to change every area of a person's heart to ... a reflection of the heart of Jesus. We could not be changed from ... e inside out or be obedient to God's ways without him. He is the ... end that you can always trust, the friend you have always dreamed ... and the friend that will never leave you or lead you astray.

... e still, small voice that spoke to me that day when I was crying ... to God for comfort is the same voice that speaks to me in every ... uation, every day that I go to him for wisdom and direction. If we ... ly yield ourselves to God and have patience to wait and then listen, ... will answer.

... e posture of humility is crucial to our receiving. We have to under... nd that we cannot do everything by our own strength, but by his ... ength, we are carried and loved and nurtured as no other person or ... ect can. We can overcome, and we can be free.

... here the Spirit of the Lord is there is freedom. I have relied solely ... the Holy Spirit in writing this book and experiencing the hearts. I ... e missed it sometimes due to distractions, but I have intentionally ... ght after God's voice and made it a priority to be present each ... to hear from him. The good news is that he comes to us again ... again with the same message of love and encouragement, even ... en we miss it. He never stops pursuing his loves. He never gives ... on us!

... the day that my daughter decided to ask Jesus to come into her heart ... receive salvation, my husband looked over on the way to church ... saw a shrub with heart-shaped clusters of flowers at a stoplight. ... had to turn around and go back to get a picture. My daughter was ... xcited to know that her Sitty and God were celebrating with her!

... e are honest with ourselves, we all desire a deeper, more authentic ... ty. We want stronger relationships with our spouse, friends, and ... ily. We desire to be full and not feel empty, alone, hurt, or forgot... We are all found in our Father and maker. He wants to add all ... eed to us, but we have to return to his heart. Finally at rest and ... ered in his mighty strength and overflowing love, we can do all ... as called us to do to help bring home his children for an everlast... eternity. We can only continue in this positive direction with the ... as our source, the most-true relationship we will ever have.

... world offers the counterfeit of this reality and lures our hearts ... from such a God and love. When we are clouded, we attempt ... uddle through the darkness. We struggle to make sense of it all, ... ging as much goodness as we can muster while balancing all of ... emands of our culture and lives. We have an enemy. John 10:10 ... s us about the enemy: "The thief cometh not, but to steal, and to ... and to destroy. . . ." This destruction can be subtle: steal your joy, ... our hope, and destroy your peace.

This scripture is clear what the goal is, but the answer and gift is the abundance of the heart of God, connected to him in relationship. Talk to the Lord just as you would a friend. Worship the Lord in all his power and glory. Read his word that brings life to everything in our world. He makes the way clear, lit, and full of his perfect love. Such actions enable us to rise above our own desires and calamity and go freely on the desires our God has put in our hearts. This age will end, and then eternity and forever will begin. What is your heart set on?

My children decided that they wanted to be baptized. We went to lunch afterward to celebrate their decisions and found a heart hanging from a car's rearview mirror parked next to us at the restaurant. All of us noticed it as we exited the car.

"Trust in You" by Lauren Daigle is a song that helped me get through writing this book. On many days, I felt ill equipped to write. My daughter and I enjoy Lauren's music so much; we find her lyrics inspiring. I would play "Trust in You" and be reminded that God, who is love, can be trusted. He knows all things all the time. When I am confused, he's not. When I am unsure, he's not. When I am impatient, he's not.

Lauren Daigle's song reminds me that when things are not moving the way I want them to and when I am wondering, he has seen it all before it happens, that the truth is that Christ has already stood everywhere I go, so I will trust in him. God's love is poured out perfectly in running, living waters, and he floods our every need as we seek him. When I think of his love, I picture a waterfall connecting to a river and the water rushing, filling the riverbed and overflowing to all of the living things around it. Its force is alive, powerful, and vibrant. It is a picture of God's love for us.

Unlike a waterfall, his love cannot be contained; it rushes and fills every dry and broken place of our hearts. Frequently, when we step out into the unknown where God has called us, something is unleashed within us. As we rely on him for every need, we are made stronger. We are confirmed in our value and purpose. We experience and know a living God. God never changes, and we can always count on him. Notice the trash around the heart found on my plate. My husband noticed it, and, at first, I said, "No, that's not a heart." Then, I looked again, and I said, "No, you're right. That is a heart!" I am so glad that even things we think aren't worth much in the world God gives purpose and value. Nothing is discarded in his eyes, which is a good lesson for us all. Sometimes we just look in the wrong places. We are never alone or forgotten. His word is alive and so is he.

My son saw a heart-shaped shell at our beach spot a few days later. Matthew 18:3 came to mind: "And said, Verily I say unto you, Except ye be converted, and become as little children, ye shall not enter into the kingdom of heaven." It is about being simple again. There is beauty and honesty in simplicity.

"CREATE IN ME A CLEAN HEART, O GOD AND RENEW A RIGHT SPIRIT WITHIN ME." PSALM 51:10

♥

While dressing for work one morning, my husband walked into the bathroom to find a heart. So delicate, so small, but not insignificant. He left it there, and then when I walked into the bathroom, I saw it. This was just a few days before my husband's birthday.

Because we are born sinners, our natural desire is to please ourselves rather than God. We can ask, however, for God to clean our hearts and give us new thoughts and desires. Good character comes from a clean heart and spirit.

I was getting my daughter ready for a father-daughter dance at her school when we had a surprise on the pathway leaving the store. We couldn't believe the heart was broken out of the concrete and filled with water, making it really stand out. I should point out that we chose to park on this particular isle, too. Out of the entire parking lot, this was in our path! It reminded me of God's faithfulness in my mom's life toward her children, arisen from her love for Christ.

I thought of how I was pouring into my daughter and teaching through the hearts about this loving, relentless God who wants hearts. The impact of a strong relationship founded on God's t changes everything in our lives for the good. God can do anyt anything at all.

A message Mom consistently taught me was the power of beauty. I think of 1 Peter 3:3–4: "Whose adorning let it not be outward adorning of plaiting the hair, and of wearing of gold, putting on of apparel; / But let it be the hidden man of the hea that which is not corruptible, even the ornament of a meek and spirit, which is in the sight of God of great price." I love this scri because while we want to have good hygiene and look nice, it sh not be our obsession. True beauty begins on the inside and s through bringing life to everything around us.

CHAPTER 10

———

HEART BEATS

♥ one.

In scripture, it is said that the Lord searches and knows every motive behind our thoughts. Sit in peace for a moment and search your heart. Do a self-check on your motives with others.

♥ two.

God's word is a lamp unto our feet, guiding us to choices that are in agreement with his precious, sweet ways and cleansing our hearts. Write a list of three things for which you are grateful.

WHAT IS GOD SAYING TO ME TODAY?

CHAPTER 11

A HEART THAT LISTENS
Receiving God's Best

God always makes the way of escape for those that seek him and have pure hearts before him. God gave my mom as a child an example of love through an aunt. Through this loving relationship, she was filled up when depleted by her circumstances. Her aunt taught her about the Lord and showed her unconditional love. This role model would help my mom become such a loving parent, showing Mom how to give unconditional love and how to teach her children about God's love for them, and providing wisdom in breaking some of the negative family cycles.

Once you have experienced things that you cannot explain, you know it's not of this world. As human beings, we are made of spirit, soul, and body. Jesus came to reconcile and make us complete in him, healing all three—spirit, soul, and body. No matter what others have done or said to us that brought hurt, we can be healed. Just like a parent on earth, he knows best, and we must be obedient in order to experience his best for us.

Alecia had prayed to God that he would show her the hearts; she felt the pain of Mom passing so soon too. I told her, "Absolutely, God is not a respecter of persons, and he knows our hearts and our needs." We don't want our hearts to be hard, not allowing God's love to penetrate the very areas that need his touch.

Soon after, Alecia texted me a picture of a heart knot in the wood of her son's play set. She had never noticed it, but as she played outside with her son, she looked up and saw it for the first time.

A few months later, she was wiping her kitchen table down after lunch and one area wouldn't dry, so she wiped it again. Then she noticed the mark was in the perfect shape of a heart. Psalm 85:8 makes clear that above any other voice listen to what God is saying, for he speaks peace to his people, the faithful ones. His glory will dw our land when we do not turn to folly but hear his voice.

We went to a family member's graduation the following summe as we were walking on the beach, there awaited a beautiful h shaped shell for us on the sand. Once again, God's timing is a perfect! The kids had been talking about Sitty again and about much she would have liked that beach. To make it even mor credible, it was on my son's birthday and my wedding anniversa Romans 10:17 scripture says, "So then faith cometh by hearing hearing by the word of God." We have to hear the word of G have faith. The word of God is who God is.

In the book *Emotionally Healthy Spirituality*, author Peter Sca writes about contemplation not only simply being about our rela ship with God. He shares that it is in the way we see ourselves other people and how we treat them. Do we see God entirely i even how he sees all people? I feel that the hearts represent G life and the ways that he communicates to us his encourager telling us that we are not alone. We just have to have eyes to My husband, Erik, and I went on a trip for my birthday and ou niversary. We picked a spot on the beach to put our things and surprised that right next to the chair was a yellow, heart-shaped We saw no other leaves of this shape, only this one.

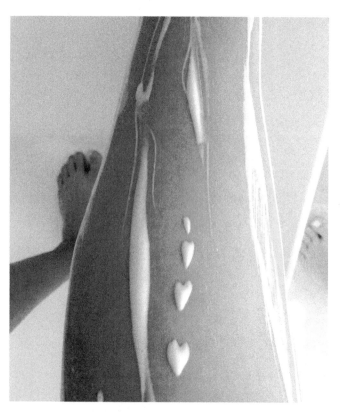

THE HOLY SPIRIT
GIVES US DIRECTIONS
AND AFFIRMATIONS TO
MAKE OUR TIME
FULFILLING AND MAKE
THE MOST OF THE TIME
GIVEN TO US.

♥

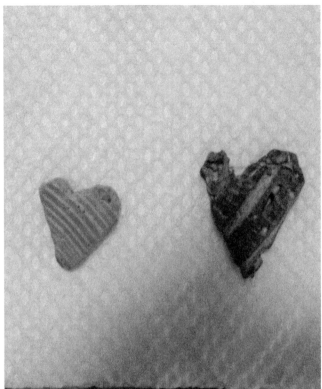

:ws 3:15 points out that while it is said, today if you will hear ice, harden not your hearts against him. My husband and I have together for twenty-six years, and he knew my mom so well. She Erik as if he were her own son. I am thankful that my husband once said no to anything regarding helping Mom. He has such ng heart and was always willing to help in any way he could. said the salvation prayer with Erik in our dating years and ht him to the Lord. Erik would frequently have long talks with about spiritual things, always learning a lot about the Bible and nature. He was always willing to listen for what God had for n those conversations.

iece was shaving her legs when the razor made a heart n in the shaving cream. She was completely overwhelmed and ned for her mom to witness what had happened. God was ing to my niece and she was listening. I'm reminded of 1 Peter hat tells us to love one another fervently with a pure heart.

tor that I have listened to for a majority of my adult life fre-ly talked about how valuable time is. It is the only thing in this that we can't get more of. You can't get it back, and you can't ore of it. He always stressed how important it is how we spend me. In Colossians, we are reminded to live wisely and to make ost of every opportunity. God redeems our time. He makes the of our time. He is the only one who can multiply our actions gh faith. We are here for a reason and a purpose. That purpose us to be a part of an invaluable love story that draws every pre-person back to the Father's heart in a world that pulls us in the site direction, if we let it.

Learning to listen to the Holy Spirit is so critical. Like in any good relationship, truly being able to listen is so vital to good communica-tion. The Holy Spirit gives us directions and affirmations to make our time fulfilling and make the most of the time given to us. Sometimes we may think there is no way and think, *I can't do that!* However, that is where we learn to hear the Holy Spirit speaking to us, relying on his strength and leading to complete all that he asks of us. We also have the demands and pulls of other people in our lives. Above all voices we need to commit ourselves to the one who gives us instruc-tion, spiritual gifts, grace, love, empowerment, and our salvation to see it through.

We can be the boxer or the punching bag. When we listen and act on what the Holy Spirit tells us, we are on the offense and choosing God's will. When we say no to God and are disobedient, however, it opens us up for the enemy's attacks. We can become the punching bag, taking blow after blow. Our choices have consequences, and God is a good Father, but we do have an enemy ready to take aim.

We need those quiet moments with God throughout our day. The beach is a place that I enjoy going to slow my pace and mind. One evening, we were at the beach to find sharks teeth and found a heart drawn in the sand. My husband found two shells in the shape of hearts. I noticed the stripped shell as I was walking up. This spot on the beach seems to be a place God speaks to us regularly. When we go, we definitely try to have a heart that listens to receive his gifts.

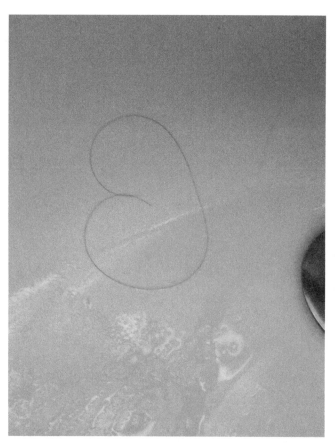

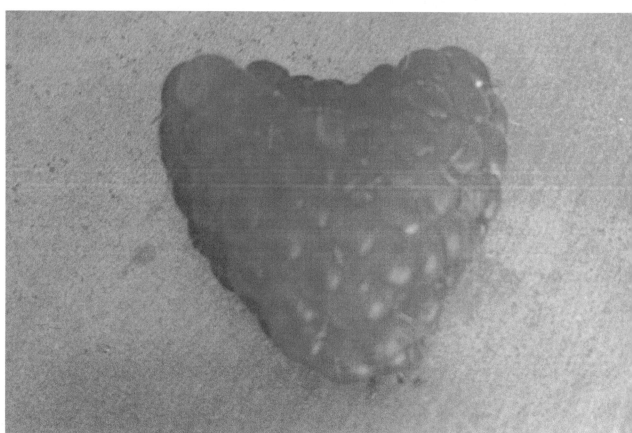

"FOR MY THOUGHTS ARE NOT YOUR THOUGHTS, NEITHER ARE YOUR WAYS MY WAYS, SAITH THE LORD."
ISAIAH 55:8

♥

I was reminded one day how God operates according to his will. I was getting dressed and looked down in the sink to see a heart-shaped strand of hair. God encourages his people no matter how crazy we think it looks! We want to fit God into our lives and our mental boxes. His wisdom and knowledge, however, are far greater than any human understanding. We must listen to him and fit our lives into his plans.

Holidays have always meant so much to my family. We went to my aunt's home for Thanksgiving where I shared the heart story with her and how God was showing his love and presence in such an incredible way to me, my friends, and our family. I went to take a bite out of a chip that I'd pulled out of a bag, and as I looked down, I saw a heart-shaped piece missing in the chip. We all were amazed! What an example of his steady presence. He had a message for my aunt, his love for her.

Weeks later, while preparing breakfast for my daughter, I pulled out a heart-shaped raspberry from the pint container. God is with the grieving. We grieve the loss here for those that go before us until we meet again. I still cannot delete my mom's name and old number from my phone. She will forever be a part of me and my family's life, until we are face to face again. We can rejoice in the fact that we will be together again. I was listening as God met us this day to touch our hurting hearts.

On the anniversary of my mom's passing, I was stopped at a stoplight and spotted a heart on a license plate ahead of me. I had been driving down the road thinking about her, about how much I missed her. She is frequently on my mind throughout my days, but more so on the anniversary of her passing. Some of the sorrow softens over time, but emotions can come flooding back at any moment. God meets us where we are and is always calling us to him. Are we tuning out the voice of this world and distractions and truly contemplating the King of Kings? Why not start today? We will never regret getting to know Jesus.

One morning, I was making pancakes for my family. I made a small pancake for my daughter. She plated it, flipping it over, and received a love note in the shape of a heart. She had a heart that listened and was present in the moment to see what God wanted to show her. Psalms 136:23 encourages us to remember the enduring nature of his royal love: "Who remembered us in our low estate: for his mercy endureth for ever." God's love runs from a well that will never run dry; it includes kindness, mercy, and faithfulness.

On the day after my birthday, late in March, I was at my son's basketball game, and my daughter, Loren, pointed out several balloons above us in the gym that we'd totally overlooked. Apparently, they'd been stuck up there since Valentine's Day the previous month. Loren was learning more and more to see and hear God everywhere. This is so important for us all. It gives us immeasurable joy to know the Father is this close.

A couple days after my birthday, I picked my spoon up from the spoon rest and found heart-shaped liquid left there. In 2 Corinthians 12:9 we are encouraged that God's grace is sufficient for us and that his strength is made perfect in our weaknesses. That is encouraging to me, that he is our strength in our times of weakness. There were many times when I was caring for Mom and my family that I felt weak and thought, *This is too much.* When I went to God, however, he gave me the strength to continue and to be the mom and wife he called me to be to my children and husband. Because of his strength, not my own, and a heart open to his I made it through with peace. First, I had to have a heart that was willing to listen.

A week later, Alecia sent me a picture of a broken goldfish that came out of the bag onto the counter. It is by his Spirit, not our own power or might. She is still working through challenging times with a blended family and establishing her relationship with her daughter. God wants us to know he is hear, and he wants to fill us with his presence. In his presence is where our hearts are filled and healed. When we start to live our lives after his heart, his lovingkindness fills our days.

In a just-because-I-love-you moment, my daughter pulled a pepper out of a salad I had just mixed and a fantastic heart was on it for her little eyes to capture. Simple yet profound. His love is bigger and wilder than we could ever imagine. It is kindness beyond human abilities, as told in Psalms 117:2: "For his merciful kinds is great towards us: and the truth of the Lord endureth for ever. Praise ye the Lord."

The next day, while at Disney World, I walked onto a ride and an awesome shell was in my path. I quickly thought, *Well, I'm sure that's just how the shells are, with hearts in them.* As I walked, I didn't see another one, though, and it was a long walk and a lot of shells. I had to go back after I got off the ride to get the picture. I realized God was showing himself and his glorious creation. I felt that the lesson for me was that sometimes we miss it in life. That's OK; the important thing to learn is to go back and make it right. And, try, try again. Have you ever heard of the saying the smartest man in the room is the one who is quiet? It is because he is listening and he is choosing his words wisely. Imagine listening to the one who has all the answers. It can save us from so much heartache.

CHAPTER 11

———

HEART BEATS

♥ **one.**

Above any other voice, the voice of peace and truth is the Father's. Identify the voices you hear and how you can align yourself with the voice of truth by writing down scriptures that speak to his truths.

♥ **two.**

We can't have hard hearts if we want to hear God's voice. Let us pray, "We entrust those painful areas of our heart that we protect, and we can be dauntlessly brave in entrusting them to you, God, and letting them be our strength as we serve openly before others.

WHAT IS GOD SAYING TO ME TODAY?

CHAPTER 12

FREEDOM UNLEASHED
In His Wholeness

Choosing to live intentionally and making decisions that require sacrifice is far from easy, but it pays off when you are turning from things that are burdens and not positive in helping you live in freedom. In God's love, total freedom comes through our obedience to his word and ways. His ways are higher than ours, and he sees the full picture of our lives. We have to relinquish our control and know an eternal creator knows what it takes to fulfill the purpose he made us for in this world and in eternity.

I heard the phrase once that the heart is the nucleus of the soul. I had no idea how God was going to reveal this to me and others in such a special way! I feel as if I've been given this sacred mystery of how to be free and give love freely. It is a mystery for all to find as they come to the feet of our King. Do I always get it right? No. Nevertheless, through the hearts, I've learned to accept others for who they are. Everyone has his or her own individual walk in life. Each person is special, and each was crafted in the secret place of a mighty Creator with his or her own special qualities for his purpose. We need to respect our differences as the human race, and even though we may not agree on things in this life, we must still have respect and love for one another. We must understand that this time is short and brief—before you know, it is gone.

Eternity is forever. Why not live and prepare for forever? It's freeing to know that no one is more special than the other is and that we all have value. However, above that knowledge, how amazing is it to comprehend that someone made us, knows every detail of our hearts, and still loves us? He was hung on a cross and totally shamed to show his love and live an example for the entire world for generations to come so that we might grasp hold of the one who created us in his image. We can be at peace simply living in the present but with an eternity mindset. The hearts represent his love for us,

love for my mom, and eternal love for those who choose it. Not the earthly-made love to which we attach strings and expectations, but the true, pure, lovely, patient, kind, and humble love!

As I have sought God's nature and truths, it has led to more jo and freedom unlike anything I've ever known! The Bible unlock profound mysteries and gives us supernatural access to the here an now—all to bring people to his heart, from the one that is fightin for them every day, our Heavenly Father!

Do you know anyone who was born with a heart that was missin some important parts or functions? Alecia's daughter has faced mul tiple heart issues since birth, having open-heart surgery four times i her first five years of life. One day, Alecia walked into her daughter room and saw paint chipped off the wall. She walked over and coul not believe what she saw: a heart for his little princess. Our Lord wil make all things new and whole. He is our comforter and healer.

God spoke these messages to my heart while writing this book: Tha he desires that his children would turn to look at him and his ways That they will see who he has created them to be, to love him an one another, bringing fullness of life in every area of their lives. Tha by being in a relationship with him, they receive and experience hi fruitfulness and consuming love.

Yes, the way of truth, love, and justice are necessary in creating ar atmosphere for us to be in relationship with God. He does not exis outside of light and truth. He is light. He is love. He is truth. He is not of flesh and bones but of the spirit realm, where we will all be one day when he returns. Until then, there are systems and order set into motion in this world since the beginning of time so that we can be in relationship with one another and share that love with one anothe

"AND GOD, WHICH KNOWETH THE HEARTS,
BARE THEM WITNESS, GIVING THEM THE HOLY GHOST,
EVEN AS HE DID UNTO US;
/ AND PUT NO DIFFERENCE BETWEEN US AND THEM,
PURIFYING THEIR HEARTS BY FAITH."
ACTS 15:8–9

♥

ng brothers and sisters home. Home is wholeness in the one ̇reated them. Love is a choice, or it wouldn't be love. It is free judgement and condemnation. His love gives us a lightness, re- ̇zes us, comforts us, gives us grace, and allows an intimacy with ̇ho knows all but is calling us to come into his fullness and rest. ̇wrote everyone's story before time. He has wonderful plans for . His plans are good and breathe freedom to our hearts and ̇but true love is an open hand and choice. Because of the fall of ̇ and Eve, we have sin, trials, and temptations, but we do have ̇rcoming spirit through the Holy Spirit when we are anchored ̇ heart. It takes us saying yes and following his lead no mat- ̇w it looks, and saying yes to uncertain actions, because that is ̇ we have to rely on him and have faith in his redemptive work, ̇g us from our wounds and learned behaviors taken on from ̇around us.

̇ith any thriving relationship, it takes us being involved and ̇ to his pursuit, leaning our ear to his guidance and carving out ̇ite moments in our day with our Father to hear his heart. He ̇ole and perfect; therefore, our hearts long for him and his life ̇ Proverbs 4:20–23 instructs us, "My son, attend to my words;

incline thine ear unto my sayings. / Let them not depart from thine eyes; keep them in the midst of thine heart. / For they are life unto those that find them, and health to all their flesh. / Keep thy heart with all diligence; for out of it are the issues of life."

Alecia was sent a heart blessing on her counter after she picked up her water glass. Jeremiah 32:27 proclaims God's supreme strength: "Behold, I am the Lord, the God of all flesh: Is there any thing too hard for me?" No matter what difficulty we are walking through, it is not too big for God. My siblings and I, including Alecia, had to deal with legal issues after Mom's passing. To say it was diffi- cult and troublesome would be an understatement. It was a dark- ness not easily comprehended and something that I probably will never understand. Thankfully, however, that is because I know Jesus. Through what was meant for evil, God drew our hearts and eyes up to him. The hearts have been a gift in many different ways and this was one big one for me and my family. It gave us our contin- ued focus on his majesty and wonder. It gave us a strong center of love and trust in Jesus as we set our eyes and faith on him, regard- less of the circumstances. We can trust him freely and his timing. We can know true freedom.

"BELOVED,
LET US LOVE ONE ANOTHER:

FOR LOVE IS OF GOD;
AND EVERY ONE THAT LOVETH IS
BORN OF GOD,
AND KNOWETH GOD.

HE THAT LOVETH NOT KNOWETH
NOT GOD;
FOR GOD IS LOVE.

IN THIS WAS MANIFESTED THE
LOVE OF GOD TOWARD US,
BECAUSE THAT GOD SENT HIS
ONLY BEGOTTEN SON INTO THE
WORLD, THAT WE MIGHT LIV
THROUGH HIM. HEREIN IS LOV
NOT THAT WE LOVED GOD,
BUT THAT HE LOVED US,
AND SENT HIS SON
TO BE THE PROPITIATION
FOR OUR SINS.

BELOVED, IF GOD
SO LOVED US,

WE OUGHT ALSO TO LOVE
ONE ANOTHER."
1 JOHN 4:7–11

♥

Many events and circumstances affect our heart in life. However, Jesus came to set our heart free from captivity, to give us a life of freedom, and to know a love that never ends or fails. The kind of love that you dream of and desire is found in a relationship with God, the Creator of the universe who knows no darkness and can only bring forth goodness and completeness. When we are anchored in Christ, know his word, and have a heart and ears to hear him, we can walk through anything, knowing that we have hope. *This life and its temporal things are not it.* Eternity is forever, and our *love* for an eternal God never ends. Everything is put right and in the right perspective in his presence. How do we know what is right and what is best for us? God said it thousands of years ago. It is the moral compass for our society. Our soul is made well and we experience the fruit of the Spirit as we follow Jesus's lead.

Making dinner one night, I cut the bad spot out of a sweet potato. Afterward, I realized there was a heart inside the spot. Colossians 3:14–15 tells us how to let charity live in our hearts: "And above all these things put on charity, which is the bond of perfectness. / And let the peace of God rule in your hearts, to the which also ye are called in one body; and be ye thankful." I feel as if this is saying that we will have conflict but we have to choose to meet each other's needs, which helps us to live in peace. God is Love—a beautiful description.

God is love and he gave his own son's life before we ever loved him. He gave up his life for people who had no love for him. I can't imagine giving up my own son, much less for people who have no affection toward him. This is the kind of love, however, that God has for his creation so that they can be coheirs with him and part of his royal family.

One morning, my husband texted a photo to me after cutting h shaving and blotting the cut only to find a heart love note insi his spilled blood, we are made whole and royal. His shed bloo us redemption and reconciliation to our Creator. Jesus did it al all we have to do is receive this freedom and love, receiving our and our place in his eternal kingdom.

We get to receive a new heart when we ask Jesus into our h Ezekiel 36:26–27 confirms our new heart: "A new heart also give you, and a new spirit will I put within you: and I will take the stony heart out of your flesh, and I will give you an heart of / And I will put my spirit within you, and cause you to walk statues, and ye shall keep my judgements, and do them." This ture speaks to our exchange for a heart that is God willed no ish willed, and with a new heart, we have God's spirit also, helps make it possible to follow what he tells us and to live l commands. How beautiful is it that not only does God repla hardened hearts but also gives us a way to overcome our struggl sins? He has it all covered and has thought out every detail to us victorious in this life.

My husband and I attended a marriage retreat based on readir book *Love & War: Find Your Way to Something Beautiful in Your riage* by John and Stasi Eldredge. At this retreat, a heart tree s was on the property as we walked through the garden. Durin retreat's closing, the leader placed a special image of two hea an easel. I thought of a phrase from Matthew 12:34: "For out abundance of the heart the mouth speaketh."

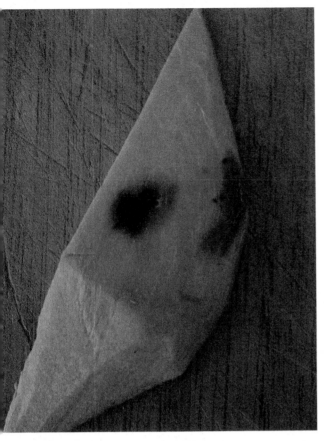

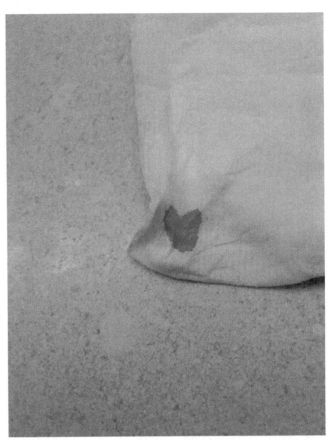

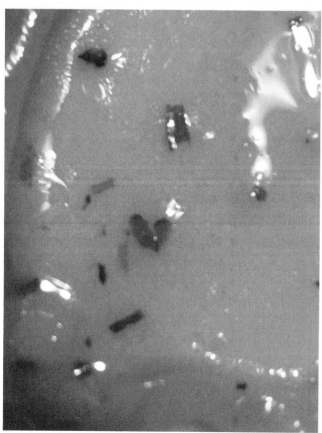
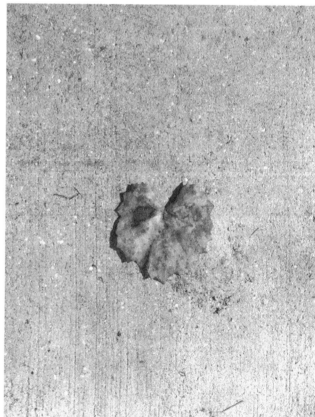

be knitted together in love, part of the greatest love story ever ... n for all of humanity! Colossians 2:2 speaks of this knitting of ...arts: "That their hearts might be comforted, being knit togeth-...ove, and unto all riches of the full assurance of understanding, ... acknowledgement of the mystery of God, and of the Father, ...f Christ." How he loves us. Lord, you take the time of every ...e to memorize me.

...ives us freedom when we are established in his love that shines ...on every dark area of our hearts and lies from our enemy to give ...oleness within. His richness and goodness is almost too much ...nprehend at times. I am thankful for the Holy Spirit, who helps ...accepting the mystery of this kind of love.

...s war! It is a war for the heart of man. True love is a choice, as I ...nentioned before. It is a choice for whom we will love, our own ...a desires or the desires of a loving Father who gives us a vast ...ity to love others and to know true love.

...mber 2015, we had a get-together with my siblings and their ...es. We went to dinner later that evening. It was just before ...tmas and we had not been all together in a long time. God had ...sage for my brother and all of us that night. A heart appeared ...brother's sandwich at the restaurant. In the doing, don't miss ...ving. It's in some of the sweet, honest conversations with our ...d loved ones that God speaks the loudest. There is freedom in ...uth and love.

...nd of my children's saw a heart shape on the side of her bowl ...r yogurt. I quickly thought of the scripture Matthew 19:14: ...Jesus said, suffer little children, and forbid them not, to come ...me: for of such is the kingdom of heaven." Jesus is saying in

this scripture that the kingdom of heaven belongs to such as these children and to let the children come to him and not hinder them. Powerful words, *and do not hinder them*. Some days it is just beyond my comprehension. I guess that is how a God should be who is not confined to our minds or our time.

We are but a speck, but yet also so miraculously formed by every intricate detail. The same week as the previous heart sighting, my daughter found a heart on her plate. Psalm 34:8 came to mind: "O taste and see that the Lord is good: blessed is the man that trusteth in him." In other versions of the Bible, it is written that *trusteth* means "refuge." We are made complete in his covering of safety—a truth that I have learned time and time again.

My sweet, brave, and strong niece encountered a heart in her path while walking home. A whisper of his love for her. God quickly spoke this to my heart after receiving my niece's picture.

Compel our hearts to you, Lord. When we start to compare with others, let us instead fix our hearts and eyes on you. Bring us closer to your love as we seek you so that we can walk confidently, in knowing that we are loved and that we have a God-given purpose. A love so strong that we want to be obedient to the things you call us to, because we know we will experience your love in even greater ways. Amen!

A few days later, my daughter was eating her breakfast and she saw a heart gift of love. She went to take a bite and could not believe her eyes. We have this confidence and freedom when he dwells in our hearts. There is no doubt in my mind that my mom is in perfect freedom now with her King. She is clothed in dignity, consuming love, and endless peace. What a beautiful joyous place to be.

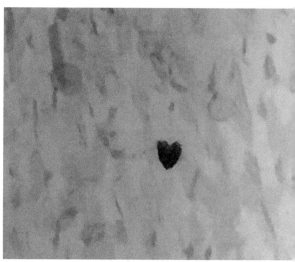

A week later, my husband was getting ready for work and noticed water formed into the shape of a heart. John 14:21 reminds us, "He that hath my commandments and keepeth them, he it is that loveth me: and he that loveth me shall be loved of my Father, and I will love him and manifest myself to him." He reveals himself to those who keep his commandments and love him. Knowing the Father is knowing freedom. Mom taught me to seek God above a religion and that his word is alive and brings us freedom, if we trust him in the process.

My husband was in an interview for a job opportunity. He looked down before it started and saw a heart next to his chair. Ultimately, he did not get the job. Again, resting in the one who knows everything and has a perfect plan. It was another reminder of his presence and faithfulness. This is freedom.

The hearts have continued even as I write this book. God woke me up in the early morning and had me write down these words:

The world is full of its own images. Images for the best in sports, most talented people, what's considered cool, what's held in most value, is current, or is beautiful, but the only image he cares about is the *image of love*, our hearts being made into his image, showing the world a beautiful, crazy kind of love that makes everything complete. Images are used in our society to cloud our vision and distract us from the one true, pure, image—Jesus.

We giving value and comparing ourselves to these images, in a sense, make idols before God. An idol is something you put first in your life before Christ. That could be food, friendships, working out, drinking, shopping, or recreational activities. All of these are good, but they shouldn't be our first response for need or fulfillment. Replacing these things for time with our Everlasting Father slowly chips away at our hearts, piece by piece. Before we know it, we are fragmented and not sure of much concerning our faith. This is the plan the enemy has every day to pull our hearts away from Christ.

At the end of the day, none of these things ever quite cure the ache. When we focus on Jesus and his attributes and turn the voice down

of the world, we will find our purpose, our value, and more th[an] ever asked for or dreamed. The images of these hearts is an ast[onish]ing view of his wild love for his children. It is God's goodne[ss] will forever live in our hearts. This is our testimony of how fa[r] vast, yet present our God is. Not just for me or my friends and but for anyone willing to seek him and have a relationship with [him.] My hope is that you have eyes to see unequivocally God's lo[ve] power moving here on this broken, hurting world, moving in yo[ur life] as you look back to see threads of his faithfulness weaving th[rough] your own ups and downs, or starting here and now by experi[encing] Jesus in your life.

The call from my doctor about my mammogram in the breathe[r chap]ter happened as I was finalizing the end stages of this book. W[e will] always be faced with challenges in this life, and at every point [he] wants us to go to him and receive his covering through them a[nd he] wants us to rise up and look up, to him, accepting his love an[d em]brace. The hearts I know will continue for me and those arou[nd me,] and I know he wants to speak to you in your own love language[. Lean] in and be ready to receive an incredible flood of his beautiful l[ove.]

The hearts are a sign and wonder from the Lord. Your sign and [won]der could be hearts or it could be something else. The first s[tep to] experiencing and leaning into God's presence is seeking him [in] your moments of talking with him. When you ask him to c[ome into] your heart, he will answer. You may not understand at first, bu[t con]tinue to seek him and learn about his ways. He will show you [step]by-step in his perfect timing.

When we ask him into our hearts is when we begin to enter int[o re]lationship with him, as he is alive on the inside of us, giving us e[ternal] life. "For God so loved the world that he gave his only begotte[n Son] that whoever believes in him should not perish but have everl[asting] life" (John 3:16). He died on the cross for those that do not [know] him. He took our sin and remembers no more. God gave hi[s] Son to have our hearts. We can have gratitude and rest in that. [When] pride, our gasp of breath, selfishness, struggles, and worries co[me we] can remember whose we are and that we have a great friend in

"FOR THIS CAUSE I BOW MY KNEES UNTO THE FATHER OF OUR LORD JESUS CHRIST,

OF WHOM THE WHOLE FAMILY IN HEAVEN AND EARTH IS NAMED,

THAT HE WOULD GRANT YOU, ACCORDING TO THE RICHES OF HIS GLORY, TO BE STRENGTHENED WITH MIGHT BY HIS SPIRIT IN THE INNER MAN;

THAT CHRIST MAY DWELL IN YOUR HEARTS BY FAITH; THAT YE, BEING ROOTED AND GROUNDED IN LOVE,

MAY BE ABLE TO COMPREHEND WITH ALL SAINTS WHAT IS THE BREADTH, AND LENGTH, AND DEPTH, AND HEIGHT;

AND TO KNOW THE LOVE OF CHRIST, WHICH PASSETH KNOWLEDGE, THAT YE MIGHT BE FILLED WITH ALL THE FULNESS OF GOD."

EPHESIANS 3:14–19

who makes us whole again while we stand vulnerable and exposed in his presence.

His beautiful story is being walked out through his beautiful people for his glorious purposes. Leave life where you walk. That's what Jesus did, and that's what he calls his people to do. It's in the fire that our King forges his most precious children, emerging more like the kingship he has created us for. We are made strong in our weakness because of Jesus. Jesus is our answer to every cry of our hearts. Jesus fills every bro-

ken, cracked, darkened area of our hearts with his glorious light. He infuses us with everlasting love that is beyond human reasoning, because it is more than just reason; it is the supernatural. The unexplainable. The miraculous. My prayer is that we are *heart to heart* with God. Royal. Loved. Forever.

Thank you, Father, for your love notes and for your love that has no bounds! I want more of you, God.

———

HEART BEATS

♥ one.

What is God calling you to do beyond your fears and insecurities? That is where we will be free and fruitful, seeing Christ in all his glory.

♥ two.

To be free in Christ's love is lacking nothing. It is being whole. The Holy Spirit leads us to the way of freedom. Listen for his voice. He is always before you.

WHAT IS GOD SAYING TO ME TODAY?

NOTES

NOTES

NOTES

NOTES

CPSIA information can be obtained
at www.ICGtesting.com
Printed in the USA
FSOW04n1029170617
35318FS